Addressing Special Educational Needs and Disability in the Curriculum: Modern Foreign Languages

The SEND Code of Practice has reinforced the requirement that *all* teachers must meet the needs of *all* learners. This book provides practical, tried and tested strategies and resources that will support teachers in making modern foreign languages accessible, challenging and exciting for all pupils, including those with special needs. The author draws on a wealth of experience to share his understanding of how SEND can affect learning and how the MFL teacher can reduce or remove any barriers to learning.

Offering strategies that are specific to the context of MFL teaching, this book will enable teachers to:

- ensure all pupils are able to participate fully in every lesson;
- develop pupils' understanding, motivation and enjoyment;
- adapt content and resources when differentiating materials for pupils with a wide range of learning needs;
- use formative assessments to measure learning.

An invaluable tool for whole-school continuing professional development, this text will be essential for teachers (and their teaching assistants) seeking guidance specific to teaching languages to all pupils, regardless of their individual needs. This book will also be of interest to SENCOs, senior management teams and ITT providers.

John Connor is former head of faculty, local authority adviser, senior examiner, AST assessor and Ofsted inspector for MFL. He is currently a trainer, author and consultant, as well as a school governor.

Addressing Special Educational Needs and Disability in the Curriculum

Series editor: Linda Evans

Children and young people with a diverse range of special educational needs and disabilities (SEND) are expected to access the full curriculum. Crucially, the current professional standards make it clear that *every* teacher must take responsibility for *all* pupils in their classes. Titles in this fully revised and updated series will be essential for teachers seeking subject-specific guidance on meeting their pupils' individual needs. In line with recent curriculum changes, the new Code of Practice for SEN and other pedagogical developments, these titles provide clear, practical strategies and resources that have proved to be effective and successful in their particular subject area. Written by practitioners, they can be used by departmental teams and in 'whole-school' training sessions as professional development resources. With free Web-based online resources also available to complement the books, these resources will be an asset to any teaching professional helping to develop policy and provision for learners with SEND.

The new national curriculum content will prove challenging for many learners, and teachers of children in Y5 and Y6 will also find the books a valuable resource.

Titles in this series include:

Addressing Special Educational Needs and Disability in the Curriculum: Modern Foreign Languages
John Connor

Addressing Special Educational Needs and Disability in the Curriculum: Music
Victoria Jaquiss and Diane Paterson

Addressing Special Educational Needs and Disability in the Curriculum: PE and Sport
Crispin Andrews

Addressing Special Educational Needs and Disability in the Curriculum: Science
Marion Frankland

Addressing Special Educational Needs and Disability in the Curriculum: Design and Technology
Louise T. Davies

Addressing Special Educational Needs and Disability in the Curriculum: History
Ian Luff and Richard Harris

Addressing Special Educational Needs and Disability in the Curriculum: Religious Education
Dilwyn Hunt

Addressing Special Educational Needs and Disability in the Curriculum: Geography
Graeme Eyre

Addressing Special Educational Needs and Disability in the Curriculum: Art
Gill Curry and Kim Earle

Addressing Special Educational Needs and Disability in the Curriculum: English
Tim Hurst

Addressing Special Educational Needs and Disability in the Curriculum: Maths
Max Wallace

Addressing Special Educational Needs and Disability in the Curriculum: Modern Foreign Languages

Second edition

John Connor

Routledge
Taylor & Francis Group

LONDON AND NEW YORK

Second edition published 2017
by Routledge
2 Park Square, Milton Park, Abingdon, Oxon OX14 4RN

and by Routledge
711 Third Avenue, New York, NY 10017

Routledge is an imprint of the Taylor & Francis Group, an informa business

First edition published 2004 by David Fulton Publishers as *Meeting SEN in the Curriculum: Modern Foreign Languages* by Sally McKeown

British Library Cataloguing in Publication Data
A catalogue record for this book is available from the British Library

Library of Congress Cataloging in Publication Data
A catalog record for this book has been requested

ISBN: 978-1-138-69927-4 (hbk)
ISBN: 978-1-138-69928-1 (pbk)
ISBN: 978-1-315-51717-9 (ebk)

Typeset in Helvetica
by Keystroke, Neville Lodge, Tettenhall, Wolverhampton

Visit the eResources: www.routledge.com/9781138699281

Printed and bound by CPI Group (UK) Ltd, Croydon, CR0 4YY

Contents

Appendices

Series authors

The author

John Connor is a former head of faculty, local authority adviser and senior examiner. He has also served as an Ofsted team inspector for modern languages and special educational needs in mainstream settings. John was also an assessor on the Advanced Skills Teacher programme for the DfE. He is currently working as a trainer, author and consultant, and has directed teaching and learning quality audits across England, the Channel Islands, Europe, the Middle East and the Far East. He is also a governor of a local primary school.

A dedicated team of SEN specialists and subject specialists have contributed to this series.

Series editor

Linda Evans was commissioning editor for the original books in this series and has co-ordinated the updating process for these new editions. She has taught children of all ages over the years and posts have included those of SENCO, LA adviser, Ofsted inspector and HE tutor/lecturer. She was awarded a PhD in 2000 following research on improving educational outcomes for children (primary and secondary).

Since then, Linda has been commissioning editor for David Fulton Publishing (SEN) as well as editor of a number of educational journals and newsletters: she has also written books, practical classroom resources, Masters course materials and school improvement guidance. She maintains her contact with school practitioners through her work as a part-time ITT tutor and educational consultant.

SEND specialist

Sue Briggs has been supporting the education and inclusion of children with special educational needs and disabilities, and their parents, for over 20 years;

variously as teacher, Ofsted inspector, specialist member of the SEN and Disability Tribunal, school improvement partner, consultant and adviser. She holds a masters degree in education, a first class BEd and a diploma in special education (DPSE distinction). Sue was a national lead for the Achievement for All programme (2011–13) and a regional adviser for the Early Support programme for the Council for Disabled Children (2014–15) and is currently an independent education and leadership consultant.

Sue is the author of several specialist books and publications including *Meeting SEND in Primary Classrooms* and *Meeting SEND in Secondary Classrooms* (Routledge, 2015).

Subject specialists

Art

Gill Curry was head of art in a secondary school in Wirral for 20 years and advisory teacher for art and gifted and talented strand coordinator. She has an MA in print from the University of Chester and an MA in women's studies from the University of Liverpool. She is a practising artist specialising in print and exhibits nationally and internationally, running courses regularly in schools and print studios.

Kim Earle is vice principal at Birkenhead High School Academy for Girls on the Wirral. She has previously been a head of art and head of creative arts, securing Artsmark Gold in all the establishments in which she has worked. Kim was also formerly Able Pupils and Arts Consultant in St Helens, working across special schools and mainstream schools with teaching and support staff on art policy and practice. She still teaches art in a mixed ability setting in her current school and works closely with local schools and outside organisations to address barriers to learning.

Design and technology

Louise T. Davies is founder of the Food Teachers Centre, offering advice and guidance to the DfE and other organisations based on her years of experience as a teacher and teacher trainer, and her role in curriculum development at QCA and the Royal College of Art. She led innovation at the Design and Technology Association, providing expertise for a range of curriculum and CPD programmes and specialist advice on teaching standards and best practice, including meeting special educational needs. Most recently, she has worked as lead consultant for the School Food Champions programme (2013–16) and as an adviser to the DfE on the new GCSE in food preparation and nutrition.

English

Tim Hurst began his career as an English teacher at the Willian School in Hertfordshire, becoming Second in English before deciding that his future lay in SEND. He studied for an advanced diploma in special educational needs and has been a SEN co-ordinator in five schools in Hertfordshire, Essex and Suffolk. Tim has always been committed to the concept of inclusion and is particularly interested in reading development, which he passionately believes in as a whole-school responsibility.

Geography

Graeme Eyre has considerable experience of teaching and leading geography in secondary schools in a range of different contexts, and is currently Assistant Principal for Intervention at an academy in inner London. Graeme is a consultant to the Geographical Association and a Fellow of the Royal Geographical Society. He has also delivered training and CPD for teachers at all levels. He holds a BA in geography, a PGCE in secondary geography and an MA in geography education.

History

Ian Luff taught in comprehensive schools for 32 years and was head of history in four such schools, writing extensively and delivering training in teaching the subject. He served in the London Borough of Barking and Dagenham as advisory teacher and as deputy headteacher at Kesgrave High School in Suffolk. Ian was made an honorary fellow of the Historical Association for contributions to education in 2011 and is currently an associate tutor and PhD student in the School of Education and Lifelong Learning at the University of East Anglia.

Richard Harris taught in comprehensive schools for 16 years, and was a head of history and head of humanities, as well as teacher consultant for history in West Berkshire. He has spent 15 years working with trainee history teachers at the universities of Southampton and Reading and is currently director of teaching and learning as well as researching issues mainly relating to history education. He has advised government bodies and worked extensively with the Council of Europe on teacher education and history education. He was made an honorary fellow of the Historical Association in 2011.

Maths

Max Wallace has nine years' experience of teaching children with special educational needs. He currently works as an advanced skills teacher at an inclusive mainstream secondary school. Appointed as a specialist leader in education for mathematics, Max mentors and coaches teachers in a wide network of schools. He has previously worked as a head of year and was responsible for the continuing professional development of colleagues. He has a doctorate in mathematics from Cardiff university.

Music

Victoria Jaquiss trained as a teacher of English and drama and held posts of English teacher and head of PSE, music and expressive arts at Foxwood School. She became a recognised authority on behaviour management and inclusion with children in challenging circumstances. The second half of her career has involved working for the Leeds Music Service/ArtForms as Steel Pan Development Officer and deputy inclusion manager/teacher. She was awarded the fellowship of the Royal Society of Arts in 2002.

Diane Paterson began teaching as a mainstream secondary music teacher. She went on to study how music technology could enable people with severe physical difficulties to make their own music, joining the Drake Music project in Yorkshire and becoming its regional leader. She then became inclusion manager/teacher at Leeds Music Service/ArtForms, working with children with additional needs. As secretary of YAMSEN: SpeciallyMusic, she now runs specialist regional workshops, music days and concerts for students with special/ additional needs and their carers.

PE and sport

Crispin Andrews is a qualified teacher and sports coach, and has worked extensively in Buckinghamshire schools coaching cricket and football and developing opportunities for girls in these two sports. He is currently a sports journalist, writing extensively for a wide range of educational journals, including *Special Children* and the *Times Educational Supplement*, and other publications such as *Cricket World*.

Religious education

Dilwyn Hunt taught RE for 18 years before becoming an adviser first in Birmingham and then in Dudley. He currently works as an independent RE adviser supporting local authorities, SACREs and schools. He is also in demand across the country as a speaker on all aspects of teaching RE, in both mainstream and special settings. He is the author of numerous popular classroom resources and books and currently serves as the executive assistant in the Association of RE Inspectors, Advisers and Consultants.

Science

Marion Frankland (CSciTeach) has been teaching for 16 years and was an advanced skills teacher of science. She has extensive experience of teaching science at all levels in both mainstream and special schools, and has worked as a SENCO in a special school, gaining her qualification alongside her teaching commitment.

A few words from the series editor

The original version of this book formed part of the 'Meeting SEN in the Curriculum' series which was published ten years ago to much acclaim. The series won a BERA (British Educational Resources Award) and has been widely used by ITT providers, their students and trainees, curriculum and SEN advisers, department heads and teachers of all levels of experience. It has proved to be highly successful in helping to develop policy and provision for learners with special educational needs or disabilities.

The series was born out of an understanding that practitioners want information and guidance about improving teaching and learning that is *relevant to them* – rooted in their particular subject, and applicable to pupils they encounter. These books exactly fulfil that function.

Those original books have stood the test of time in many ways – their tried and tested, practical strategies are as relevant and effective as ever. Legislation and national guidance has moved on however, as have resources and technology; new terminology accompanies all of these changes. For example, we have changed the series title to incorporate the acronym 'SEND' (special educational needs or disability), which has been adopted in official documents and in many schools in response to recent legislation and the revised Code of Practice. The important point to make is that our authors have addressed the needs of pupils with a wide range of special or 'additional' needs; some will have education, health and care (EHC) plans which have replaced 'statements', but most will not. Some will have identified 'syndromes' or 'conditions' but many will simply be termed 'low attainers'; pupils who, for whatever reason, do not easily make progress.

This second edition encompasses recent developments in education, and specifically in modern foreign languages teaching. At the time of publication, education is still very much in an era of change; our national curriculum, monitoring and assessment systems are all newly fashioned and many schools are still adjusting to changes and developing their own ways forward. The ideas and guidance contained in this book, however, transcend the fluctuations of national politics and policy and provide a framework for ensuring that pupils with SEND can 'enjoy and achieve' in their MFL lessons.

NB: The term 'parent' is used throughout and is intended to cover any adult who is a child's main care-giver.

Linda D. Evans

Acknowledgements

The author would like to thank the following for kindly granting permission to reproduce their content in this book:

Erszi Culshaw, a Spanish teacher, and Rachel Smith of Ramsey Grammar School, Isle of Man, for providing case study material.

Saira Ghani at Chiltern Edge School for giving permission to use a screenshot from her blog, www.chilternedgemfl.typepad.com, in Chapter 3.

Storybird for permission to use an image from a picture book, *Quand il fait du vent*, created by the author (www.storybird.com).

David Evans of Fox Lane Photography.

Staff and pupils of St John's CofE Middle School in Bromsgrove and Queensbury School in Erdington for allowing us to use photographs of their pupils in this publication.

Crick Software for use of screenshots from their Clicker 7 software in Chapter 3 (www.cricksoft.com).

Introduction

Ours to teach

Your class: thirty individuals to teach – to encourage, motivate and inspire; thirty individuals who must be seen to make good progress regardless of their various abilities, backgrounds, interests and personalities. This is what makes teaching so interesting!

Jason demonstrates very little interest in school. He rarely completes homework and frequently turns up without a pen. He finds it hard to listen when you're talking and is likely to start his own conversation with a classmate. His work is untidy and mostly incomplete. It's difficult to find evidence of his progress this year.

Zoe tries very hard in lessons but is slow to understand explanations and has difficulty in expressing herself. She has been assessed as having poor communication skills but there is no additional resourcing for her.

Ethan is on the autistic spectrum and finds it difficult to relate to other people, to work in a group and to understand social norms. He has an education, health and care plan which provides for some TA support but this is not timetabled for all lessons.

Do you recognise these youngsters? Our school population is now more diverse than ever before, with pupils of very different abilities, aptitudes and interests, from a wide range of cultures making up our mainstream and special school classes. Many of these learners will experience difficulties of some sort at school, especially when they are faced with higher academic expectations at the end of KS2 and into KS3–4.

Whether they have a specific special educational need like dyslexia, or are on the autistic spectrum, or for various reasons cannot conform to our behavioural expectations – *they are ours to teach*. Our lessons must ensure that each and every pupil can develop their skills and knowledge and make good progress.

How can this book help?

The information, ideas and guidance in this book will enable teachers of languages (and their teaching assistants) to plan and deliver lessons that will meet the individual needs of learners who experience difficulties. It will be especially valuable to subject teachers because the ideas and guidance are provided within a subject context, ensuring relevance and practicability.

Teachers who cater well for pupils with special educational needs and disabilities (SEND) are likely to cater well for *all* pupils – demonstrating outstanding practice in their everyday teaching. These teachers have a keen awareness of the many factors affecting a pupil's ability to learn, not only characteristics of the individual but also aspects of the learning environment that can either help or hinder learning. This book will help practitioners to develop strategies that can be used selectively to enable each and every learner to make progress.

Professional development

Our education system is constantly changing. The national curriculum, SEND legislation, examination reform and significant change to Ofsted inspection means that teachers need to keep up to date and be able to develop the knowledge, skills and understanding necessary to meet the needs of all the learners they teach. High quality continuing professional development (CPD) has a big part to play in this.

Faculties and subject teams planning for outstanding teaching and learning should consider how they regularly review and improve their provision by:

- auditing

  a) the skills and expertise of current staff (teachers and assistants);
  b) their professional development needs for SEND, based on the current cohorts of pupils;

  (An audit proforma can be found in the eResources at: www.routledge. com/9781138699281)

- using the information from the two audits to develop a CPD programme (using internal staff, colleagues from nearby schools and/or consultants to deliver bespoke training);

- enabling teachers to observe each other, teach together, visit other class-rooms and other schools;
- encouraging staff to reflect on their practice and feel comfortable in sharing both the positive and the negative experiences;
- establishing an ethos that values everyone's expertise (including pupils and parents who might be able to contribute to training sessions);
- using online resources that are readily available to support workforce development (e.g. www.nasen.org.uk/onlinesendcpd/);
- encouraging staff to access (and disseminate) further study and high quality professional development.

This book, and the others in the series, will be invaluable in contributing to whole-school CPD on meeting special educational needs, and in facilitating subject-specific staff development within departments.

1 Meeting special educational needs and disabilities

Your responsibility

New legislation and national guidance in 2014 changed the landscape of educational provision for pupils with any sort of 'additional' or 'special' needs. The vast majority of learners, including those with 'moderate' or 'mild' learning difficulties, weak communication skills, dyslexia or social/behavioural needs rarely attract additional resources: they are very much accepted as part of the 'mainstream mix'. Pupils with more significant special educational needs and/or disabilities (SEND) may have an education, health and care plan (EHC plan): this outlines how particular needs will be met, often involving professionals from different disciplines, and sometimes specifying adult support in the classroom. Both groups of pupils are ultimately the responsibility of the class teacher, whether in mainstream or special education.

> High quality teaching that is differentiated and personalised will meet the individual needs of the majority of children and young people. Some children and young people need educational provision that is additional to or different from this. This is special educational provision under Section 21 of the Children and Families Act 2014. Schools and colleges *must* use their best endeavours to ensure that such provision is made for those who need it. Special educational provision is underpinned by high quality teaching and is compromised by anything less.
>
> (SEND Code of Practice: DfE 2015a)

There is more information about legislation (The Children and Families Act 2014; The Equality Act 2010) and guidance (SEND Code of Practice) in Appendix 1.1.

Definition of SEND

A pupil has special educational needs if he or she:

- has a significantly greater difficulty in learning than the majority of others of the same age; or
- has a disability which prevents or hinders him or her from making use of facilities of a kind generally provided for others of the same age in mainstream schools or mainstream post-16 institutions.

(SEND Code of Practice: DfE 2015a)

The SEND Code of Practice identifies four broad areas of SEND (see Table 1.1), but remember that this gives only an overview of the range of needs that should be planned for by schools; pupils' needs rarely fit neatly into one area of need.

Whole-school ethos

Successful schools are pro-active in identifying and addressing pupils' special needs, focusing on adapting the educational context and environment rather than on 'fixing' an individual learner. Adapting systems and teaching programmes rather than trying to force the pupil to conform to rigid expectations will lead to a greater chance of success in terms of learning outcomes.

Table 1.1 The four broad areas of SEND

Communication and interaction	Cognition and learning	Social, emotional and mental health difficulties	Sensory and/or physical needs
Speech, language and communication needs (SLCN)	Specific learning difficulties (SpLD)	Mental health difficulties such as anxiety or depression, self-harming, substance abuse or eating disorders	Vision impairment (VI)
Asperger's Syndrome and Autism (ASD)	Moderate learning difficulties (MLD)		Hearing impairment (HI)
	Severe learning difficulties (SLD)	Attention deficit disorders, attention deficit hyperactivity disorder or attachment disorder	Multi-sensory impairment (MSI)
			Physical disability (PD)
	Profound and multiple learning difficulties (PMLD)		

Guidance on whole-school and departmental policy making can be found in Appendix 1.2 and a sample departmental policy for SEND can be downloaded from www.routledge.com/9781138699281.

Policy into practice

In many cases, pupils' individual learning needs will be met through differentiation of tasks and materials in their lessons; sometimes this will be supplemented by targeted interventions such as literacy 'catch-up' programmes delivered outside the classroom. A smaller number of pupils may need access to more specialist equipment and approaches, perhaps based on advice and support from external specialists.

The main thrust of the Children and Families Act and Chapter 6 of the SEND Code of Practice is that outcomes for pupils with SEND must be improved and that schools and individual teachers must have high aspirations and expectations for all.

In practice, this means that pupils should be enabled to:

- **achieve their best**; additional provision made for pupils with SEND will enable them to make accelerated progress so that the gap in progress and attainment between them and other pupils is reduced. Being identified with SEND should no longer be a reason for a pupil making less than good progress.
- **become confident individuals living fulfilling lives**; if you ask parents of children with SEND what is important to them for their child's future they often answer 'happiness, the opportunity to achieve his or her potential, friendships, and a loving family' – just what we all want for our children. Outcomes in terms of well-being, social skills and growing independence are equally as important as academic outcomes for children and young people with SEND.
- **make a successful transition into adulthood, whether into employment, further or higher education or training**; decisions made at transition from primary school, in Year 7 and beyond should be made in the context of preparation for adulthood. For example, where a pupil has had full-time support from a teaching assistant in primary school, the secondary school's first reaction might be to continue this level of support after transition. This may result in long-term dependency on adults however, or limited opportunities to develop social skills, both of which impact negatively on preparation for adulthood.

Excellent classroom provision

Later chapters provide lots of subject-specific ideas and guidance on strategies to support pupils with SEND. In Appendix 1.3 you will find useful checklists to help you support pupils with identified 'conditions' but there are some generic approaches that form the foundations of outstanding provision, such as:

- providing support from adults or other pupils;
- adapting tasks or environments;
- using specialist aids and equipment as appropriate.

The starting points listed below provide a sound basis for creating an inclusive learning environment that will benefit *all* pupils, while being especially important for those with SEND.

Develop pupils' understanding through the use of all available senses by:

- using resources that pupils can access through sight *and* sound (and where appropriate also use the senses of touch, taste and smell to broaden understanding and ensure stronger memory);
- regularly employing resources such as symbols, pictures and film to increase pupils' knowledge of the wider world and contextualise new information and skills;
- encouraging and enabling pupils to take part in activities such as play, drama, class visits and exploring the environment.

Help pupils to learn effectively and prepare for further or higher education, work or training by:

- setting realistic demands within high expectations;
- using positive strategies to manage behaviour;
- giving pupils opportunities and encouragement to develop the skills to work effectively in a group or with a partner;
- teaching all pupils to value and respect the contribution of others;
- encouraging independent working skills;
- teaching essential safety rules.

Help pupils to develop communication skills, language and literacy by:

- making sure all pupils can see your face when you are speaking;
- giving clear, step-by-step instructions, and limiting the amount of information given at one time;
- providing a list of key vocabulary for each lesson;
- choosing texts that pupils can read and understand;

- making texts available in different formats, including large text or symbols, or by using screen reader programs;
- putting headings and important points in bold or highlighting to make them easier to scan;
- presenting written information as concisely as possible, using bullet points, images or diagrams.

Support pupils with disabilities by:

- encouraging pupils to be as independent as possible;
- enabling them to work with other, non-disabled pupils;
- making sure the classroom environment is suitable, e.g. uncluttered space to facilitate movement around the classroom or lab; adapted resources that are labelled and accessible;
- being aware that some pupils will take longer to complete tasks, including homework;
- taking into account the higher levels of concentration and physical exertion required by some pupils (even in activities such as reading and writing) that will lead to increased fatigue for pupils who may already have reduced stamina;
- being aware of the extra effort required by some pupils to follow oral work, whether through use of residual hearing, lip reading or signed support and of the tiredness and limited concentration which is likely to ensue;
- ensuring all pupils are included, and can participate safely, in school trips and off-site visits.

These and other, more specific strategies are placed in the context of supporting particular individuals described in the case studies in Appendix 1.4.

2 The inclusive MFL classroom

A teacher at The Priory School, a secondary school for pupils with moderate learning difficulties and autistic spectrum disorders, in Lincolnshire, shares his experience of working with pupils with special needs:

> This fenland countryside is very sparsely populated and the effects of rural deprivation are all too apparent. Many of our pupils have very limited experience or understanding of the world outside their immediate home area. We decided to go camping in France and offered the visit to all our Year 9 pupils, most of whom leapt at the chance. The visits that year and the two years following were a great success, both in terms of the educational experience for the pupils and educating ourselves. However, at the end of one of those weeks, one of our pupils, Lucy, said to her teacher on the ferry home, 'Miss, those French people are really clever, aren't they?'
>
> When asked why she thought this, Lucy replied, 'Well, Miss, we've learned a bit of French and it was really hard but those French people all speak it really well!'

Lucy's comment really brought into focus one of the key issues involved in teaching a foreign language to pupils with learning difficulties – even at the age of 14, she had still not fully grasped the idea that people in other countries grow up learning a mother tongue that is different from English (Howes 2001).

Figure 2.1

There are many children in many parts of the country – and not necessarily children with learning difficulties – who have little sense of the world outside their own particular community. Part of the role of all teachers, not just teachers of modern foreign languages, is to give pupils that sense of the wider world and their own place in it. This was confirmed for me early on in my career, when, on a cross-Channel ferry to Boulogne, a Year 8 girl, visibly anxious, asked me, 'Sir, how will we know when it's our stop?'

Why teach MFL to pupils with special needs?

MFL teachers will be familiar with the arguments for and against teaching additional languages to pupils with special needs. One of the avowed intentions of the DfES (2002) publication *Languages for all: Languages for life, a strategy for England* was that 'secondary pupils should have high quality teaching and learning at Key Stage 3 and a flexible curriculum and range of routes to support success during the 14–19 phase'.

Some pupils with special needs excel at modern foreign languages as this account of lessons with pupils on the autistic spectrum shows:

> French is a popular subject in the communication disorder unit at Hillpark Secondary in Glasgow . . . the pupils have many strengths in favour of language learning. Good rote memory, for example, is ideal for vocabulary learning. Youngsters are keen on routine and this, coupled with a lower level of self-consciousness about speaking out, works well with greetings and instructions in French classes. This lack of self-consciousness brings an added ability to repeat accurately and mimic speech, so a good French accent can develop naturally.
>
> (Caldwell 2002)

In similar vein, David Wilson, head of equal opportunities and modern foreign languages at Harton School, suggested that MFL can enhance rather than detract from literacy:

> Our SEND pupils are very indignant if we attempt to withdraw them from MFL lessons. They want to remain with their friends, enjoying what they see as a fun and practical activity. German has a relatively simple spelling system and over the years I've known many young people getting better GCSE results in German than in English . . . Starting from scratch in another language might well be the making of them and lead to an improvement in their mother tongue performance.
>
> (Wilson 2003)

Many pupils enjoy learning a language, especially in the early stages and find it exciting and rewarding. It has status and is seen as being something of a rite of passage, as pupils move up through school. The advent of compulsory languages in Key Stage 2 reinforced the value of language learning. The Key Stage 2 Framework for Languages (DfES 2005: 47) stated:

Learning a language is of value to the majority of children with special educational needs. Experience has shown that these children enjoy their language learning experience and improve their overall achievement as a result. In particular children make progress in these areas:

- linguistic development;
- social development;
- cultural awareness;
- self-esteem.

The document further states that:

Learning even the rudiments of a new language enables children to extend and develop linguistically and demonstrate new skills. Examples of such development include improvement in pronunciation, progress in reading and listening skills, and growing awareness of language in general by providing opportunities to reinforce and revisit first language concepts. Evidence suggests that children can operate in a new language at the same conceptual and linguistic level as their own language; this ease of transference promotes general linguistic development.

(DfES 2005: 49)

These points are reinforced in the aims of the new curriculum:

The national curriculum for languages aims to ensure that all pupils:

- understand and respond to spoken and written language from a variety of authentic sources;
- speak with increasing confidence, fluency and spontaneity, finding ways of communicating what they want to say, including through discussion and asking questions, and continually improving the accuracy of their pronunciation and intonation;
- can write at varying length, for different purposes and audiences, using the variety of grammatical structures that they have learnt;
- discover and develop an appreciation of a range of writing in the language studied.

The emphasis is clear in the opening statement – 'to ensure that *all* pupils . . .'.

The view that learning a language can enhance rather than detract from general literacy was further reinforced by the report published in 2012 by

CfBT (Tinsley and Comfort 2012). Paragraph 3.3, Literacy and first language development, states:

> Popular opinion often questions the advisability of teaching a foreign language 'when children have difficulty mastering their own', or suggests at least that literacy in the first language is the priority and second language learning, while perhaps desirable in its own right, is somehow a separate and less pressing issue. This section provides evidence not only of the many ways in which second language learning supports literacy in the first, but also of the added-value of second language study in providing opportunities to learn about language in general.

There is extensive literature linking mother tongue and second or foreign language development, traceable back to Vygotsky's observation from the 1930s that a child's understanding of his or her native language is enhanced by learning a foreign one:

> The child becomes more conscious and deliberate in using words as tools of his thought and expressive means for his ideas . . . The child's approach to language becomes more abstract and generalized . . . The acquisition of foreign language – in its own peculiar way – liberates him (sic) from the dependence on concrete linguistic forms and expressions.
>
> (Vygotsky 1930)

So SEND pupils in primary schools are enjoying meaningful language learning experiences thanks to the thoughtful interventions of skilled teachers, as seen in this document elaborated by Erszi Culshaw, a peripatetic teacher of Spanish in Lancashire.

My successful strategies in teaching Spanish to primary children with SEND

ASD

- We avoid getting too loud when we play games; we make sure we can keep our voices low (hot/cold hiding games or games when we have to change our voices).
- When using puppets, I always say that they just *pretend* to talk, as the children with ASD will insist that they can't talk and will be confused.
- I always use the same soft toy – a parrot – to throw to pupils at the beginning of the lessons for question/answer time: if I lose it temporarily I just pretend to throw this parrot, as other objects are confusing for them (like a cat, because cats don't fly).

(Continued)

- I give a clear structure of the lesson in English for them to know what is going to happen next.
- I don't insist on them joining in activities where they have to read emotions or they have to say how they are feeling as they find identifying feelings confusing.
- When it comes to taking turns in role plays, I stand behind them and help out; they can find social interactions difficult.
- I stick to the same routine in my lessons whenever I can; children with ASD like routine and change can result in behavioural problems.

ADHD

- I make sure the pupils know the structure of the lesson.
- I try to avoid activities with too much excitement.
- I do my best to give very simple and clear instructions.
- I let them 'fiddle' if they are not distracting their classmates.

Speech delay

- The pupils respond well to songs and classroom routines; I make sure the lesson has lots of repetition with songs and repetitive elements.
- I never force anyone to speak in the TL or in English. I try to make sure they feel safe and confident.

Selective mutism

- I try to increase confidence of the pupils by including them in activities where they don't need to speak to participate, e.g. they can point to an object or a word in the display. I try to make sure they feel safe.
- I don't expect or push them to talk.

Basic good practice

Children with special educational needs can find language learning very challenging and so we must make every effort to ensure that they are given as much support as possible. In order to accommodate the varying needs of pupils, a range of strategies will be required, but basic good practice goes a long way to making the curriculum accessible to all pupils.

There are many practical things which a teacher can do to make life easier for the learner. Remember to make everything explicit:

- Establish routines for opening and ending the lesson: '*Bonjour*' . . . '*Au revoir*'.

- Tell them what you expect: that they will speak in the target language, repeat phrases aloud, listen to one another and do homework.
- Model, explain, practise and reinforce routines.
- Avoid 'sandwiching', i.e. immediately following the target language with its English translation: '*Abrid los libros* – open your books – *página veintiocho* – page 28'. The net effect of this is that pupils filter out the target language because they know the English is coming along any minute.
- Try encouraging some pupils to act as 'interpreters' who can pass on your instructions to the class, but only after you've finished giving them in the target language.
- Tell them what they have to bring to each class: do not assume they will bring pen, pencils, coloured pencils, paper, etc. Teach them the words for these and check regularly. Display a list of required 'equipment' on the wall (with images) so that they can see the words as well as hear them.
- Be clear about when students have choices and what the choices are, e.g. *Il y a cinq questions. Répondez aux trois.*
- Be clear which things are not optional, e.g. *Écoutez dans le silence.*
- Plan for appropriate social interaction. How will pair work and group work be incorporated? Careful partnering can make a big difference to pupils with SEND, for example a pupil with a sight impairment may have a well-developed auditory memory. He can be teamed up with pupils who are good wrihters but lack confidence in oral work. In this way, both parties benefit.
- Be clear about when speaking is good and when it is a distraction.
- Establish norms for noise level in the room, and educate the pupils about this level so that they can take responsibility. Do not shout as this just adds to the noise and confusion. Flick the light switch on and off as a signal that you want the class to be quiet. Not only will this save your voice but also it will attract the attention of pupils with a hearing impairment and those who find it hard to listen.

The atmosphere

Put the group at ease. Emotional support is particularly important in the MFL classroom where pupils may be nervous about learning in a totally new context. Everyone learns best when they are relaxed and feel safe, but language learning, to a certain extent, depends on taking risks. Pupils are encouraged to reach out for unfamiliar words and sounds, and children, especially adolescents, are reluctant to do this if they feel they will be laughed at. The emotional environment within the classroom, then, is particularly important, and teachers need to ensure that pupils are expected to be supportive of one another. Praise pupils who help one another and show good active listening skills. An overt and planned approach to teaching a phoneme–grapheme relationship can be extremely useful in developing pupils' ability to attack unfamiliar words without undue interference caused by using mother tongue pronunciation on foreign words (see Erler and Prince 2012). This will help develop their confidence and reduce exposure to being laughed at.

Use time effectively: structure the lesson so that learning comes in manageable chunks. Provide a structure so that pupils process language and do not just parrot it.

A useful model is:

- **PRESENT the language to be learned**.
  Explain it and show it. Use colour on the board to bring out key points. Make sure pupils have a handout or have time to copy it down. They need to see, hear and understand. Give slow writers and pupils with sensory impairments a copy of the text so they are working on comprehension, perhaps with a learning support assistant, instead of wasting time copying text very slowly and inaccurately.

- **PRACTISE the new structure or vocabulary.**
  This means using repetition and question and answer to get pupils to repeat the language in the same context in which it was presented. This can work well in the context of a story rather than in unstructured, unrelated examples. For example, if you are teaching the future using *aller* + infinitive, you might link to daily routines: *Demain André va se lever à sept heures. Il va manger . . . .*

- **EXTEND the language practice to new contexts.**
  This might draw on previous knowledge or vocabulary from other topics. Once you are confident that pupils understand the structure of *aller* + infinitive, extend it to: *Demain André et sa soeur Hélène vont rendre visite à . . .*

- **PREPARE for communication.**
  Pupils undertake tasks to help them reinforce knowledge. Move away from the story to more varied examples and wider contexts such as holidays, when I leave school, etc.

- **PUPILS COMMUNICATE.**
  Here pupils make independent use of the new language. Set a task – written or oral – but make it clear that you are assessing their ability to use the form *aller* + infinitive.

Never split the explanation from the practice. Always put grammar and new vocabulary near the beginning of a lesson. If you teach something one lesson and wait till next time to put it into practice, the pupils will have forgotten.

Encourage pupils to develop their curiosity and problem-solving skills. Build a success culture: keep promoting your subject. Be positive, communicate high expectations – that everyone can and should make progress in their language learning. Celebrate their achievements but be honest – don't praise without justification, as pupils will see through that and feel patronised. Some pupils have learned to be helpless, because they have spent much of their life being dependent on adults. They expect parents, siblings, teachers, LSAs and other pupils to make decisions, direct activities and sort out problems. Offer praise for everything that they achieve independently. It may not be a long piece of work or of high quality, but it may be their first solo endeavour and that is worth celebrating. The work of Carol Dweck, professor of psychology at Stanford University, may well be of benefit in this regard (see Dweck 2012). She has elaborated the concept of 'growth mindset' to combat this learned helplessness. Pupils are encouraged to link achievement with effort, rather than innate ability. Praise is judiciously and sparingly given, as over-praising a piece of work can be counterproductive – the pupil thinks 'Oh, I'm good at this, so I don't have to work at it.' The approach is to develop into a 'not yet' teacher. When a pupil says 'I don't get it' the instinctive answer should be 'Not yet, but let's find out what's stopping you.' The other useful example to explore with pupils is James Nottingham's 'Learning pit' (www.jamesnotting-ham.co.uk/learning-pit/), which can be used to underline the fact that learning comes about as a result of struggle, and can often involve failing. A. P. J. Abdul Kalam's definition of 'FAIL' as an acronym for 'first attempt in learning' can be helpful, as can his interpretation of END (effort never dies) and NO (next opportunity). For pupils whose self-esteem can be very low, these messages can be powerful (see www.goodreads.com/quotes/1015959).

Managing behaviour

Problems in a mixed-ability class may not be about physical disability or learning difficulty. Often they are more nebulous – the child who won't try, the child with attitude. Pupils with behavioural difficulties come in all shapes and sizes and no single strategy will work for all. Table 2.1 shows some characteristics which you may recognise from pupils in your class.

Harnessing the power of new technologies could be very helpful in positive behaviour management, and an application such as 'Classdojo' gives real-time feedback on behaviour and attitudes to work during lessons which can be linked to a rewards system. It can be customised to promote any positive behaviour characteristics or attributes at the discretion of the teacher, for instance participation, teamwork or just plain hard work. It has other useful features, such as the ability to send instant text messages to parents, or share the good moments from lessons via photographs or video clips. It can be used across different platforms such as IOS, Android and PC (www.classdojo.com/en-gb/).

Table 2.1 Some pupil behaviours

Pupil behaviours	Think about
Anti-authority, disruptive, aggressive, swearing, bullying, often out of control	The teacher who is an authority figure is like a red rag to a bull. Shouting, issuing orders, always teaching from the front of the class, using sarcasm, will bring out the worst in these pupils. Go for calm reason. Do not negotiate or change your mind about sanctions.
Unco-operative, clever, calculating, hurting others with their cruel comments	Pupils need to be kept busy to see the relevance of what they are doing to the real world. They want 'street cred' and a sense of achievement on their terms. Sometimes if they do the work, they could well be on the gifted register in some of their subjects.
Attention-seeking, manipulative	These pupils need more action and less listening, more experimentation and problem solving. If they feel rewarded and respected, they can calm down and behave in a more acceptable way which enhances their self-respect.
Unable to sit still, poor attention span, don't finish tasks, difficulty getting organised, easily distracted	Variety of tasks needed. Rewards for keeping on task. Allow them to walk around if vital but try to stop them disrupting others. Use multimedia to capture attention.
Socially isolated, procrastinating, excessively sluggish, difficulty getting started, keep to themselves socially, sensitive to criticism, moody	Pair work could be a good strategy but make these students responsible for getting work done and reporting back.
Depressed, withdrawn, anti-social to rest of class, nervous of new experiences, shy	Pupils in this group often like the immediate feedback that drills and skills activities can provide.

Of course, thinking about individual pupils and their needs is quite different from dealing with a child who is just one in a class of 30 who all want something different from the teacher. But this case study about Sarah shows what can be done.

Sarah: Year 7

Sarah has a diagnosis of Asperger's Syndrome but her academic achievement so far has been below the average for her age. Sarah had behavioural difficulties at primary school but these have not surfaced since the transfer to secondary. Rather, she has been quiet, withdrawn and anxious, drifting away from the few friends she had in her previous school. Sarah appears to be articulate, but her comprehension of both spoken and written English is poor.

She is working on the topic of *En Famille*. The French teacher needs to make the curriculum relevant and interesting, to differentiate the work so that Sarah can achieve success, and to encourage her to take part in the class as she gains more confidence. Sarah has five hours' support time on her statement of special educational needs. The school uses these hours flexibly to give her support when it is most needed. She had individual support in French for the first term as it was expected that she would find the subject difficult. However, Sarah had no major problems and she obviously enjoyed the subject. As none of the class had studied French before, Sarah quickly realised that she knew as much as anyone else and managed to keep up in class. All the staff had an INSET on autistic spectrum disorders before Sarah transferred. The teacher makes sure that Sarah has written down the homework task and understands what she has to do before she leaves the lesson.

Lesson 1 of the topic: Members of the family and negatives

Class objectives

To ask and answer questions about the names and number of family members, including answers using negatives.

Support plan* target addressed in this lesson

Sarah will put up her hand and wait when she wants to answer a question.

The lesson

Sarah chose to sit at the front of the class at a single desk by the window. She was reluctant to join in the class activity that started the lesson – flashcards of an imaginary family – but the teacher asked her several direct questions and she was able to answer, albeit in a very quiet voice.

(Continued)

The pupils then drew and labelled their own family tree. The teacher had put a note in Sarah's homework diary after the previous lesson, asking her to bring in photographs of her family, as she finds drawing very difficult. Sarah stuck these photographs into her book and wrote captions below, some words being copied from the whiteboard.

The teacher paired Sarah with another girl for the next activity, each girl asking and answering questions about the other's family. The teacher had provided prompt cards for the pairs to use (see Figure 2.2). Sarah used these and also pointed to the photographs in her book. The lesson finished with another flashcard game around the class, again about the imaginary family. Sarah was more confident this time and put up her hand twice, answering the question correctly each time.

Note

* The 2015 Code of Practice does not refer to IEPs (individual education plans), but does encourage schools to plan for targeted support.

Figure 2.2 Prompt cards for pair work

The physical environment

Factors which militate against an inclusive classroom include poor materials, misunderstandings, lack of communication and inappropriate teaching methods. The layout of the classroom is another key aspect. Look at the layout of the room and consider how you could improve it. Is it easy for the class to work in pairs without having to move lots of furniture? Is there an area that can be used for role play? Is there a quiet area? Look at equipment. Is anyone using a laptop for access? Megan is in a wheelchair and uses a laptop to help record her work. She needs to be within easy reach of a power point as her battery may well go down. Do pupils have access to tablet computers? Are you able to mirror your work and theirs via a tablet onto a big screen? This can be an important tool in developing critique and peer assessment. Do you have access to a visualiser? This can be used for the same purpose.

Often the room is full of equipment – realia, maps and pictures – and, while this can provide a visually stimulating environment, it can also provide sensory overload, particularly for any pupils with autistic spectrum disorders. These youngsters can find it difficult to concentrate in the face of even minor distractions. Make one corner a stimulus-free area where people can sit and think or engage in quiet study. Make sure that this is not seen as 'the naughty corner', but a place where pupils routinely go to work alone or in pairs.

Sit at a table in your classroom and look at the language environment from a pupil perspective:

- Have you covered every square inch of wall space with pupil work as a way of celebrating achievement?
- Do wall displays link to particular parts of the curriculum?
- Have you remembered that font size and clarity are important if texts are to be read from various points in the classroom by pupils with a visual impairment and by pupils who are struggling with the demands of the language?
- Could you add an area where pupils can write on the wall, using washable whiteboard material or a roll of self-adhesive blackboard?
- Could they, or you, write on the windows with chalk pens?
- Do you utilise the backs of chairs to display support material like lists of question words or opinion language?
- Can you use the ceiling to display support material?
- Can you display support material on the risers of the staircase leading to the department, or any nearby staircase?

Bhavini has limited sight. The class were looking at a display with photos and magazine articles about a spectacular concert in Barcelona, featuring some of their favourite artists. She stayed sitting at her desk as she knew she would not be able to see it. At break, the teacher asked Steven if he would like to earn a merit by staying behind and showing the display to Bhavini. As he has behavioural problems he was quite surprised that he had been chosen. He explained each picture to Bhavini and read out some of the text. Once or twice when he struggled to read a word, she helped him, as she has a better vocabulary and knowledge of the language. Together they made sense of the display and enjoyed helping each other.

Change displays often. They lose their appeal quite quickly. Encourage pupils to make things for the wall. They often remember things they have touched and constructed much more clearly than pieces of writing. Perhaps take a theme for a wall and use it as a stimulus for all years, for example create a character on the wall. Pupils may use this for simple things such as name, age: *Pierre a dix ans*, etc., as a focus for adjectives and descriptions, or for negatives: *Mme Dupont n'est plus jeune*. Pupils can create narratives which might focus on themes such as holidays or going to the doctor, or on more outlandish topics such as witnessing a bank robbery, which could reinforce questions, imperatives and numbers. Younger pupils will see the language work of older classes and may be able to guess at some of the words, while older pupils will be revisiting some structures and simple vocabulary when they see what pupils in Year 7 have created.

Interactive whiteboards

Interactive whiteboards have been relatively useful tools for language work because:

- It is easier to integrate sound and video as part of the lesson. This can more clearly demonstrate the relationship between the written word and what is heard.
- Colour and pictures capture learners' attention.
- The printout facility can help to reinforce messages and encourage peer discussion. Printouts are especially useful for pupils with dyslexia, who copy inaccurately and may have short-term memory problems.

However, they are not a universal remedy for all pupils. There are a number of issues which affect pupils with special needs:

- Classrooms are not always designed for interactive whiteboards so they may not be well sited.
- Can all pupils see clearly? Do you need to make sure that a child with a visual impairment is not being dazzled?
- Research suggests that the whiteboard leads to a faster pace of lesson and this may not suit those who need time for ideas and vocabulary to sink in.
- You can only engage a limited number of pupils at any one time. They're not truly interactive, because a good number of the class will be passively observing what one or two pupils are doing at the board.
- Much of the material produced for interactive whiteboards is little more than electronic versions of worksheets with limited appeal.

Making print materials more accessible

Most of the materials you use in the MFL classroom are likely to be paper-based. MFL books are generally lively and fun with lots of busy pictures, cartoons and illustrations. They work well for the majority of pupils because the text is broken up into bite size chunks so they do not get bored or lose their place. However, this style of presentation can be a problem for some learners with dyslexia and those who have particular eye conditions. If you talk about 'the picture in the bottom right corner', hold the book up and show the class where it is. Often pupils with dyslexia have particular problems with left and right and may spend ages puzzling over the wrong picture.

Illustrations are a vital ingredient, whether they are photographs, drawings or cartoons. They motivate most pupils, and in many cases give visual clues to the accompanying text. This is helpful to all learners, especially those who have a strong visual memory; illustrations also 'break up' text into more manageable chunks.

Many pupils find reading difficult for a whole variety of reasons. The majority of texts are still black print on a white background, and this is uncomfortable for some categories of readers. Pupils with dyslexia may use a coloured plastic overlay to obviate the problem of 'glare'. However, they still may find it harder to write on white paper. Schools could ease this problem by making paper available in a range of colours for homework or 'best work'.

Producing your own materials

Table 2.2 provides some guidelines for creating handouts.

See Appendix 2.1 for examples of good and not-so-good worksheets.

Use of digital recordings

Digitally recorded work may be accessible to all children in your class, but if so, bear in mind the following points:

- If a child is recording answers with a Perkins brailler, you will need to pause the recording so that the child has the opportunity to write their answer without clattering keys over the next bit of dialogue (sighted children would write their answer silently as they hear it).
- Alternatively, the visually impaired child could whisper their answer to their support assistant who would then write it down. This works particularly well for tick box questions. But again, you will have to make judicial use of the pause button to allow the child to whisper their answer without missing out on crucial dialogue.
- A sighted child and a visually impaired child could work as a pair, using the same method as above, but taking it in turns to answer the question.

Many visually impaired children have well-developed memory skills and team games can capitalise on this, using the sight of a sighted child, and the oral and listening skills of a blind or partially sighted child to report back.

Table 2.2 Creating handouts

Fonts	Arial, Comic Sans, Sassoon and New Century Schoolbook are easier to read than other fonts.
Font size	12 or 14 is best for most pupils.
Font format	**Bold** is OK; *italic* is hard to read.
Spacing	Use double or 1.5 line spacing to help pupils who have problems with visual tracking.
Layout of materials	Use lots of headings and subheadings as signposts.
CAPITAL LETTERS	These are hard to read so use sparingly.
Consistency	Ensure instructions and symbols are used consistently.
Provide answers	If pupils can check answers for themselves, they learn more and become more independent.
Enlarging	It is better to enlarge text by using a bigger font on a word processor than by relying on the photocopier. Photocopied enlargements can appear fuzzy and A3 paper never fits neatly in exercise books or folders.
Forms	If you are making an identity card or something similar, remember that partially sighted pupils often have handwriting that is larger than average, so allow extra space on forms. This will also help pupils with learning diffculties who have immature or poorly formed writing or are still printing.
Spacing	Keep to the same amount of space between each word. Do not use justified text as the uneven word spacing can make reading more difficult.
Alignment	Align text to the left margin. This makes it easier to find the start and finish of each line. It ensures an even space between each word.
Columns	Make sure the margin between columns clearly separates them.
Placing illustrations	Do not wrap text around images if it means that lines of text will start in different places. Do not have text going over images as this makes it hard to read.

Supporting writing

Many pupils find writing of any kind onerous. It requires concentration, often the ability to work for quite a long period, to remember sets of instructions, to come up with ideas, to recall the language and how to structure it, to remember spellings, then the fine motor skill to write it down. It may possibly require the pupil to then check, edit and alter it, even to rewrite – by which time he or she may be thoroughly bored with it and/or tired out. For pupils who have literacy problems in their first language, writing in a foreign language can be very daunting.

Think about motivating pupils. Keep written activities short. It is better for them to write six phrases on different topics which 'grab' them than to struggle through half a page on a subject that has no appeal.

There has been a lot of work carried out in primary schools around 'talk for writing'. This is especially valuable for pupils with SEND (of all ages) as it helps them to formulate their ideas and identify words they want to use before actually putting pen to paper. Role play or simply using 'talk partners' will help pupils to plan what each is going to say or write. Warm up games can also be useful, e.g. give pupils a word or provide a focus such as a picture or object and ask them to write down as many words as they can think of that are associated with it – individually or in pairs. Time them (perhaps a minute only) and then as a class, brainstorm as many words and ideas as possible.

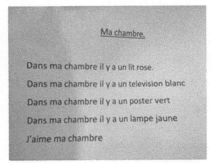

Cloze can be a useful activity. The teacher chooses a passage, removes some of the words and draws a line in each gap. The reader has to fill in the missing words. You can make the activity easier by listing all the missing words at the bottom of the page so that pupils simply have to understand the text and choose the most appropriate word to make sense of the passage.

Writing a summary can also be an accessible activity for pupils who struggle with writing. One way of starting this activity is for pupils to read through the text and then write a few questions for others to answer. The writing of the questions increases understanding and confidence in handling the text. Give them some vocabulary to get them started. You could make it a whole-class activity to generate a suitable list.

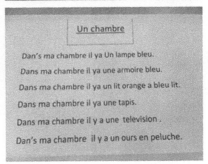

Figure 2.3 Work posted on a modern languages department blog

© Saira Ghani/Chiltern Edge School

Students should be taught the language of opinion so that they can say what they think about a topic under discussion. They should also be shown real writing, such as simple advertisements in the target language, captions and emails. They need to know languages are for life, not just for school!

Pupils are more motivated to write if there is a real purpose and a real audience for their written work apart from your red (green/blue?) pen. There will be more on this subject in a later chapter, but in Figure 2.3 you will see an example of a modern languages department blog featuring work by a low ability group. The task was to produce a 3D model of their bedroom and then write a few sentences describing it. The teacher has taken digital photographs of the models and the pupils' writing and posted them on the blog.

Multi-sensory language learning

We may have a hundred and one reasons to explain why pupils do not learn: 'He doesn't work hard enough', 'She has a disruptive home life', 'He is disorganised', 'She is deaf', 'He is dyslexic', 'She's never in school'. What we don't know most of the time is how people do learn. No one is born knowing a language. Certainly some pupils have an aptitude for language learning: some find reading easy, some are good at acquiring new vocabulary, or seem to assimilate syntax effortlessly, or have a good accent, or find ways of linking new knowledge to previously learnt material. But what makes knowledge stick? Certainly the more channels we use in teaching, the more likely we are to help pupils learn. Many pupils are very artistic, creative and imaginative, so these characteristics can be exploited in language learning:

- Pupils may have a strong eye for colour – vocabulary could be blue for masculine, red/pink for feminine. Some teachers use different colours for different tenses.
- Grammar may be an alien concept. Do not assume pupils understand singular/plural. Try to reinforce this pictorially. Not all children will understand the concept of a past tense. BSL and some community languages do not have a separate form for things which happened in the past. Give an explanation and an example, and put it into practice at once. Learning needs to be in small chunks, with lots of repetition at regular intervals. Remember: 'Children are not slow learners but they are quick forgetters.'
- When learning set phrases, chanting may be helpful as the rhythm can act as a reinforcement. Encourage pupils to make up songs (with actions) to familiar tunes such as 'Here we go gathering nuts in May'. This can help embed lots of new vocabulary, as in the hypochondriac's song:

    ♪ Bonjour Monsieur, J'ai mal à la tête, mal à la tête, mal à la tête,
    Oh Monsieur, J'ai mal à la tête! Oh la la la la!
    Bonjour Monsieur, J'ai mal à la gorge! . . .

- Set the scene – get pupils to envisage what sort of language is likely to come up. If two people are meeting for the first time, we can expect greetings, names, etc. If a passage has the word *gare*, we can look out for numbers, times and destinations.
- Talk about the country and the culture to make it all more interesting, e.g. tell them that in France, children leave their shoes out in the hope of getting presents for *la Fête des Rois*.
- Humour helps. Most children cannot understand the funny cartoons thoughtfully provided by authors of MFL textbooks, but print out a Simpson strip from the Web and they will try very hard to work out the meaning. It's funny, it's relevant, and they have a context for the language.
- Use sound. Teachers can make a digital recording with explanations of key grammar points. On a tablet computer this can be shared by using apps like ShowMe. Content can be mirrored on a large screen using AppleTV. A pupil can listen to it again and again. Or make a demonstration using alternatives to PowerPoint such as Prezi, Glogster, HaikuDeck or ExplainEverything. Then they can look, listen and maybe interact with the slides. It is sometimes claimed that a student with dyslexia needs to 'overlearn' material up to 30 times before it becomes properly implanted.
- There are software packages and interactive Web 2.0 tools such as WordTalk, VozMe, Voki and Text2Speech which enable pupils to type in what they want to say and then hear their text spoken in a range of languages. Linking word and sound helps with some pupils' learning. Simple clip art type pictures can reinforce vocabulary.
- Use art. Pupils can learn by doing. Use an art package to create adverts or posters, or apps such as DrawingDesk or AnimationDesk. One useful activity is to teach body vocabulary through drawing. Get pupils to draw a monster and describe it: *Tiene tres ojos amarillos*, *un nariz azul*, etc.
- If possible have a foreign cookery day, working with recipes in the target language.

In one imaginative project pupils from a special school were given a 'virtual' trip to France. The staff created an 'aircraft' in a classroom, with seats in rows of three. Pupils were given a 'boarding card' and a 'passport'. They sat in their seats. The plane 'took off' and the pupils were shown an 'in-flight movie' about Paris. One of the staff became a 'trolley dolly' and walked backwards down the aisle dispensing drinks and light snacks. The plane 'landed' and they all went through 'passport control' and into the hall, where the staff had set up a mock town square. The pupils had various tasks to carry out, such as change money, buy and write a postcard, buy a drink and a snack, buy a souvenir. For each task carried out successfully their passport was stamped. The shops were staffed by Year 10 pupils from the local comprehensive school. Prizes were awarded to the pupils with the most stamps, although in reality everybody 'won' something – best accent, fewest mistakes, etc. After an hour or so, they made their way back to the 'airport' and boarded the 'plane' again. In the intervening period, the staff had gone back to the 'plane' while the pupils were in the hall and turned all the seats round so that they were facing in the opposite direction. When asked about this, they explained that the children were now flying back, so they would need to see that the plane was going in a different direction. Such attention to detail can make learning experiences more powerful and memorable for the pupils.

Remember that your main objective is to make pupils confident in their ability to understand and communicate. So this chapter ends with an anecdote. A coach trip to Spain stopped for a break at a service station some miles south of Paris. Many of the adults held back and muttered among themselves, not daring to try and buy anything as it would involve speaking French and they might lose face. A boy with Down's syndrome stepped forward and asked for *'deux croissants et un café s'il vous plait'*. He then emptied out his pockets, scattering notes and small change in several currencies. The cashier helped him pick it up, extracted the right money and he was on his way with his food. The adults went hungry whilst he enjoyed his breakfast. What excellent communication and life skills! His teacher could be very proud.

3 Teaching and learning

I am an NQT in MFL who trained in a school with set classes. My new school has mixed-ability groups. How can I ensure that every pupil's learning needs are catered for, in particular those with SEND? Differentiating tasks tends to mean that planning my lessons can take a very long time. Is there any advice on how to effectively plan and teach lessons to the benefit of all pupils in a mixed-ability teaching group?[1]

An inclusive classroom is very hard to define but it is about developing the least restrictive environment. Not every child is going to be able to do all the four competencies of speaking, listening, reading and writing equally well. It is very much about differentiation and enabling pupils to show what they can do instead of what they can't. But it needs a change in mindset by some teachers, from believing that differentiation is something 'extra' to do, for which they don't really have time; to understanding that it is an integral part of any good lesson.

> Developing differentiated learning has meant an evolution in the role of the teacher from a simple imparter of knowledge to a multi-skilled professional who leads and guides groups and individuals towards their peak. Many aspects of differentiation require us to challenge our comfort zones and move away from the security and safety of whole class routines; but creating new working practices . . . can make students feel more comfortable when they find they are more engaged and can make better progress.
>
> (Anstee 2011)

One of the first things that teachers need to realise is that a mixed-ability group means exactly what it says: the group has a mixture of abilities. This is quite different from seeing the class as a group of average and able children, with a subset of children who have problems. Pupils have all sorts of strengths which can be exploited to benefit one another. A pupil with a visual impairment may have poor spelling and be slow to produce written work but may have a fantastic aural memory and a wonderful capacity to absorb and speak the language.

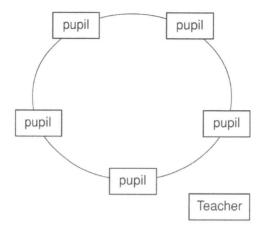

Figure 3.1 Classroom model for a mixed-ability group

A child with limited hearing may find it hard to reproduce the sounds needed for French, German or Spanish, but may have developed a host of study skills for decoding meaning from unfamiliar words and find it easy to transfer these skills to other languages. All pupils can learn from each other. The classroom model should be as shown in Figure 3.1.

The teacher is not the central focus but rather a guide, time keeper and resource provider to help learning take place effectively. This role may mark a change for some teachers who fear they will lose control if they adopt more learner-centred styles of teaching.

Learning

People learn in different ways and, in the past, schools focused very much on a reading and writing approach to grammar and vocabulary. Through research on literacy and thinking skills, we have come to realise that there are many different routes to the same goal. Yet often this does not transfer to classroom practice. Some pupils simply do not learn if they are sitting down! Somehow movement stimulates the brain. Yet pupils are constantly told to stop wandering about the room and get back to their seats.

In 1981 Roger Sperry won the Nobel Peace Prize for his experimentation on left-brain and right-brain hemisphere brain functions. He discovered that most of us use both sides of our brain, but have a bias to one side or the other. According to Sperry, traditional academia is very left-brained with an emphasis on words, details and categorising. The right side of the brain focuses on non-verbal and intuitive ways of working (see Table 3.1).

The origins of this theory may well date from studies in the 1950s on patients whose brains had been surgically split to treat their intractable epilepsy. But for people whose brains are intact with both hemispheres in continuous and

Table 3.1 Left- and right-brain learning styles

Left brain emphasises	Right brain emphasises
language	images
rules and grammar	awareness of shape
mathematical formulae	appreciation of patterns
numbers	ability to work in three dimensions
sequences	rhythm and musical appreciation
linearity	seeing the whole picture
analysis	

co-ordinated communication, the distinctions between left and right brain are irrelevant to performance.

It might seem at first glance as if only traditionally academic, left-brained children are going to make a success of their language learning, but we know that is not true. Otherwise, every school would have hundreds of right-brained children who are totally unable to communicate in their first language. Many children, if stimulated with appropriate prompts, make an enormous leap in language acquisition. They are no better or worse than left-brained children; they just have different strengths and weaknesses.

A good teacher needs to be flexible. Some learners will benefit from pictures and flashcards. Put up part of a picture on a whiteboard and get pupils to call out what they think it is (see Figures 3.2 to 3.5). You will be pleasantly surprised at how much language knowledge they demonstrate. This gives you the chance to improve their pronunciation and endings if necessary while praising them for the effort.

Figure 3.2 Qu'est-ce que vous voyez? Blanc? Bleu? Lignes? Oui. Brosse? Très bien – une brosse . . .

Figure 3.3 Alors qu'est-ce que vous voyez? Une brosse aux dents. Oui et . . . oui, c'est le dentifrice.

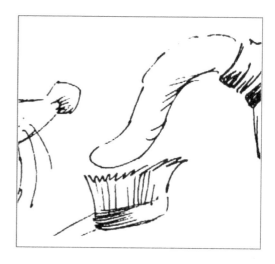

Figure 3.4 Et maintenant? Oui, c'est un animal. Un lapin? Peut-être . . .

Figure 3.5 Ah non, c'est une souris.

See Appendix 3.1 for more pictures.

At this point, it is important to introduce a caveat. While recognising that pupils access knowledge in different ways, it has become evident that nailing one's colours to the mast of so-called 'learning styles' has become counterproductive. There is no real evidence that theories such as Visual-Auditory-Kinaesthetic

(VAK) make any significant difference to pupils' outcomes (Riener and Willingham 2010). In fact they are often referred to as 'zombie' theories – dead but they won't lie down. Pupils do have preferences, but in the long run they make no difference to their ultimate performance. Theories such as multiple intelligences and Brain Gym have also been discredited and as such should be approached with caution.

'Talking dice' is a popular product for improving and developing speaking and listening skills. With each throw of the dice, pupils are encouraged to let their imaginations roll. One set of pupils used them to discuss where they went on holiday; another for talking about things they liked and disliked, giving reasons. Teachers report that it encourages random, spontaneous language which works well for vocabulary, grammar, sentence building, story telling and discussion (Anstee 2011). See www.talkingdice.com/video.htm. There is also a free app for smartphone and tablet: Talking Dice 3D (see https://itunes. apple.com/gb/app/talking-dice-3d/id569487370?mt=8&ign-mpt=uo%3D4). Another useful resource is the card game 'Kloo', which helps pupils with sentence structure (see www.kloogame.com).

Develop pupils' listening and speaking skills by providing digital recordings to take home to learn vocabulary or structures. Make sure that those who prefer to learn by touching and doing get enough physical activity, perhaps by manipulating chunks of language on cards or by miming activities to fix a connection between their action and the language being learned. This is a lot of work, but you will find that once you have a range of resources for different KS3 and KS4 topics, they can be re-used. Even more importantly, you will develop a different way of thinking so that often it becomes second nature to think of different ways of revisiting the same points. Once you have created the right range of resources, which tap into pupils' different aptitudes, you will enable them to work independently. See Appendix 3.2 for useful resources.

Teaching strategies

Pupils will come into the room with all sorts of other things in their head. Concentration may be better in the morning than in the afternoon when they are getting tired. Alternatively, some classes are very sluggish during the first period. Some pupils may find it difficult to settle down on Monday mornings after the weekend. Sometimes they are 'on a high' after a particular lesson such as drama.

There needs to be some sort of active learning in each lesson, whether it is writing or a tactile activity or a role play or multimedia work. Pupils need to see it, hear it, say it, touch it, taste it or smell it. Languages lend themselves to auditory exercises or visual games, to role play, pair work and group work.

Languages can incorporate number work, poetry, advertisements, football scores, map work, songs and whole-class chanting. Resources like websites, YouTube film clips, newspapers and magazines taken from the language's country of origin can be especially useful.

Set routines and expectations. Ensure that students know what they are supposed to 'pull out of their bag'. If you have a short, sharp activity to work on it will help to settle them down and focus attention, as well as providing a reason to get out pens and exercise books.

It might be that each lesson pupils have to note the date and the weather. If you are working on food then for three weeks perhaps they need to write down at the start of each lesson what they had for tea the previous night. On the other hand, the tasks might change.

'List 6' is a useful quick starter. Here the pupils have to make a list of six things. These might be colours, things you would take on a picnic, items in your suitcase, school subjects or parts of the body. Those with limited language skills should be encouraged to produce a minimum of three things. This task should be accomplished quickly. It should set the pace of the lesson, tune pupils into the language and get them to focus. It is a 'doing', rather than a listening or looking activity. Other activities are listed in Appendix 3.3.

Good practice guide

- Where possible try to incorporate some reading, writing, speaking and listening in each lesson. This could just be a few words or sentences but it is important to cover as many of the different skills as possible.
- Offer the students a choice of activities if possible. Some pupils are good at learning from a book or worksheet; others learn by speaking a language.
- Encourage all students to highlight words or phrases they are unsure about and make them active participants in the learning process.
- Talk about how students will find the answer (apart from asking you!). Can they guess the word? Do they know a similar phrase? Can they make sense of the sentence without that word? What does it say in the glossary? Can they find it in the dictionary or by using Wordreference.com on a mobile device?
- Remember the aim is to give them strategies to cope when they are faced with a similar situation in real life, and there's no teacher to hand.

Good direct teaching is achieved by balancing different elements:

Directing	Sharing teaching objectives with the class, ensuring that pupils know what to do and drawing attention to points over which they should take particular care. Make sure the pace of the lesson is brisk but not too fast.
Instructing	Giving information and structuring it well in small chunks. Ensure practice follows instruction to embed language and concepts.
Demonstrating	Showing pupils what to do, modelling the language and giving clear examples.
Explaining and illustrating	Showing what a good response is and why. Where possible try to link to previous work so pupils have hooks to hang new learning on.
Questioning	Using open and closed questions; questioning in ways which match the direction and pace of the lesson and ensure that all pupils take part. Give examples and remember to say the pupil's name before asking the question, to alert him and give him every chance of providing a good answer. Build in 'thinking time', rather than expecting an immediate response.
Discussing	Responding constructively to pupils; ensuring that pupils of all abilities are involved and contribute to discussions, allowing pupils time to think through answers before inviting a response. Think about altering the seating arrangements to facilitate discussion.
Consolidating	Finding opportunities to reinforce and develop what has been taught, through a variety of activities in class and well-focused tasks to do at home.
Feedback	High quality formative feedback which moves pupils on. Teach them the principles of peer assessment and critique as part of developing a 'growth mindset'. The YouTube clip 'Austin's Butterfly' with Ron Berger is a good example of pupils learning how to critique each other's work in a spirit of constructive criticism.
Plenary	Ask the question: 'What do you know/can you do that you didn't know/couldn't do before today?' and get members of the group to offer suggestions.

Finishing off

Use the final five or ten minutes of your session to consolidate the group learning. Re-cap your main aims with additional examples, and try to find an imaginative way to assess outcomes for individuals. One approach is to get pupils to discuss in pairs what they think they have learnt that day, how it links to previous work and what they need to remember. Alternatively, choose one or two pupils to be the 'expert' and take questions from the rest of the class. Pupils spend a few minutes preparing a question for the experts. Doing this helps them focus on the purpose of the lesson and provides good feedback for the teacher.

Differentiation by resource

There are very few MFL teachers who just rely on a textbook. These days it is easy to get hold of materials from magazines, digital recordings, videos, travel books, CD-ROMs and websites (see Figure 3.6). The real question is: how do you decide what to take into the classroom?

Ideally, you need real objects for pupils to touch and handle and talk about: *La jupe est verte. Elle est longue.* The whole process then becomes concrete and multi-sensory as pupils see and touch the object, and hear and speak the language. However, it is not always possible to take in real objects for each

Figure 3.6 Concentration may be better in the morning than in the afternoon
© Foxlane Photos

lesson. Pictures help for all sorts of reasons. They remove the translation process. If a pupil sees an item and thinks of it in a second language then a link is made, but if he is always thinking of English words and translating them into the target language there is a barrier to learning.

Symbols and pictures can make difficult concepts visible and therefore easier for pupils to understand. Pupils need a context. Lots of struggling readers can decode words once they know what they are looking at. If they see a picture of a football match, they can start to make guesses about unfamiliar vocabulary, such as *le terrain*, *marquer un but*, *l'arbitre*.

But do choose pictures carefully. Relevance and clarity are crucial – they need to enhance text rather than distract. Make sure that pictures are near enough to the relevant passage, but not so near that they encroach on white space. Not all pupils are graphically literate and, while you may think that the picture is self-evident, it may be too busy for the pupil to pick out the message. Think about what you want the picture to do. Is it just to set the scene and provide a context? Is it to tell a story, or to provide an imaginative stimulus for extended writing, or is it to illustrate particular words and phrases? For a pupil such as Susan, who has communication and language difficulties, the picture of a bedroom does not conjure up the idea of furniture and describing your own or an ideal bedroom. It suggests bedtime stories, and you may find yourself off at a tangent with the 'Three little pigs'. By the time you have digressed into '*Les trois petits cochons*', you may be off on animal vocabulary, and have lost the thread of your lesson (see Figure 3.7). It is often assumed that pupils respond better to pictures than to words: 'One picture is worth a thousand words'. Just remember that for some pupils that is at least 900 too many!

Make sure you select resources with appropriate reading levels. One simple test is to choose an exercise or passage of about six lines. If there are more than ten words the pupil doesn't know or can't remember, the work is too

Figure 3.7 'One picture is worth a thousand words'

hard. Often realia such as menus and packaging can be very attractive, but the text may not be accessible to some pupils. Make sure that labels on diagrams, maps and illustrations do not cross the lines of the drawing. This deprives the word of its recognisable shape. Even changes in colour or texture under a word can make it more difficult to read.

A checklist for evaluating materials

And finally – a checklist based on work by some Lancashire support teachers will help you look at course content and resources when differentiating materials for pupils with a wide range of learning needs.

Checklist for evaluating materials

Content

- Can the core content be reduced?
- Is it easy to extend it?
- Is there an appropriate alternative to this core?

Layout

- Can work be spread out over more pages?
- Is work in clear print, e.g. word processed in a sans-serif font?
- Are there line breaks in appropriate places?
- Could there be more emphasis on key words?
- Is sufficient white space used?

Vocabulary

- Can you provide a word bank for revision/introduction of core vocabulary?
- Have you got a further vocabulary list for increasing the complexity of discussion and recording?
- Are there any extra opportunities to practise using/reading/spelling the new vocabulary in a motivating context?
- Do you provide opportunities to revisit essential vocabulary?
- Do you offer creative as well as analytical activities for using vocabulary?

Reading

- Could there be a simpler version?
- Are there opportunities for more illustrations?

- Would symbols add meaning? Could these be developed by the class?
- Could content be digitally recorded or videoed?
- Can pupils work in pairs so that competent readers can help others?
- Is text in electronic format? Text to speech software could be used.
- Are there extra resources (CD-ROMs, reference books or websites at a variety of levels, extension worksheets) for strugglers and quick finishers?

Figure 3.8

© Foxlane Photos

Matching tasks to student abilities, aptitudes and interests

Students work in a variety of ways and bring different abilities and aptitudes to that work. One form of differentiation is to provide a variety of tasks that cover the main content area in order to cater for the variety of individuals in the class.

Food vocabulary can be covered in different ways: through vocabulary lists, exercises in a book or formal instruction. Alternatively, the same vocabulary can be covered by drawing out the most relevant vocabulary for pupils by getting them talking: devising menus, discussing their own eating habits, etc.

Sample lesson

Teaching food vocabulary and preferences

1. Make a list of about 40 different foods with pictures.
2. Children choose foods they like or dislike.
3. Make a preferences sheet, as shown below. This will vary according to the abilities of the children. One group will just select foods and put them in two columns: *j'aime, je déteste*; other groups will have extra structures to use.

Group 1	Group 2	Group 3
J'aime	+ mais je préfère	+ je n'aime pas
Je déteste	+ J'adore	+ mais je ne déteste pas non plus

Letting children choose their own foods does run the risk that they will not cover all food areas. Many may lack fruit and vegetables! But it will be real and, by letting them pick food words for themselves, they invest more time and thought in the process and are more likely to remember.

In one lesson pupils were using the 'Play sandwich maker' from the Early Learning Centre. This consists of a plastic loaf with slices stuck together with Velcro, a plastic knife to 'slice' the bread and slices of cheese, ham, lettuce and tomato, all with Velcro tabs. The teacher had set up the conceit that they were running a sandwich shop and that customers had emailed their orders in. These were on a printed sheet for the pupils to consult. They then had to make up the 'sandwiches' according to each order (reading comprehension – did the sandwich match the written order?). There was also a supply of white paper bags available for the pupils to use. They had to write the type of sandwich on the bag (copywriting for accuracy of spelling, correct word order, legible handwriting) and place the sandwich in the bag for the teacher to assess. Did the writing on the bag accurately reflect the contents? This process enabled all pupils to participate and enjoy success.

Building learning routes

Improve pupils' word recognition skills by creating wordworms on the computer by running words together and removing accents and punctuation. Even better, get them to create wordworms for others. Pupils have to recreate the text by working out where words begin and end. This involves close reading

Figure 3.9 A Clicker grid
© Crick Software

and is a good test of comprehension and grammar skills. It's an excellent collaborative exercise:

Jaimelesframboisesmaisjedetestelespommes

Let them learn by looking and listening. Use a 'Clicker grid' that combines pictures with sound. Click on the illustration and you can hear the word in English or French.

The Clicker grid set shown in Figure 3.9 enables pupils to make their own onscreen book about animals in French. Each page contains a picture and a words pop-up, enabling pupils to write about each animal, using the construction *C'est un/une . . . .* (This activity works best with a French speech engine, available from Crick Software. Pupils can read a ready-made version of the book, using the set 'Les Animaux – Read'.)

The Clicker grid set shown in Figure 3.10 is designed to reinforce knowledge and recognition of number words from 1 to 10 in Spanish.

Use drama strategies to enliven learning. Pupils mime actions to a simple narrative told by the teacher. Use simple props to create a character – a waiter, a businessman in a hurry. Create a setting: a half-eaten meal is on a table. What can we deduce about this person from the clues? Is it a man or a woman?

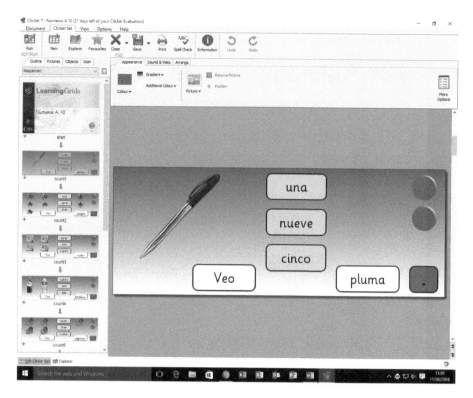

Figure 3.10 Numeros A 10
© Crick Software

Age? Lifestyle? Pupils respond to the same task but at different levels and perhaps in pairs or groups.

Alter the setting for your teaching – not all learning takes place in a classroom. Key Stage 3 pupils from a school in Coventry worked on a French food project with a special needs teacher. These pupils required high levels of support and had made least progress with the language. They visited a supermarket and took digital photographs of fruit displays etc., and they went to the local market to take photographs of stalls and cafés. They used a multimedia package to combine these pictures with recordings of their voices and that of the French *assistante*: '*Voici les oranges*', '*J'ai deux pommes*', and so on.

After three weeks they rejoined the main group to find that their vocabulary was considerably wider and their pronunciation better than the rest of the class. They had also made a resource for the MFL department which was widely admired and this made them feel useful and valued.

This exercise may be difficult to replicate with a large group but certainly time spent in a real-life situation, perhaps with an LSA or a language assistant, is very worthwhile. Many towns have a French market for a few days each year and if it is not possible to take the whole class, you could see if the market holder would come to the school to talk for a small fee.

A range of tasks to allow choice

When designing tasks, it is important to allow for different starting points for pupils' varying abilities. Remember also to provide variety in type, level, media, skills and styles. Engage creative as well as analytical strategies for decoding and recall. Letting pupils choose the tasks that they carry out will enable them to develop their differing aptitudes and interests. Encourage plenty of consultation to minimise pupils' making unsuitable choices. Encourage as much participation as possible in both planning and instruction.

Cut a simple narrative into sections and ask pupils to organise it into a sequence that pleases them. They could then add illustrations and create their own book. Compare versions made by the class and consider which are more successful and why. These adapt well to working on a computer screen, where the finished documents can then be printed. Simple cut and paste techniques allow for re-arrangement of the text, and the undo facility allows for retracing steps.

Analytical and creative activities

There are various ways of revisiting vocabulary. You could get the pupils to divide food into things they eat at home and things they buy outside:

Chez moi	*J'achète*
pommes de terre	frites
la viande	le poisson
le fromage	pizza

You could ask them to choose eight to ten of their food words and put them on a continuum from breakfast to dinner, thinking about when in the day they are most likely to eat them, e.g.:

pain grillé, du café, les oeufs, les saucissons, du fromage, frites, du riz, du vin, gateau

Le petit déjeuner -

Le déjeuner -

Other pupils could put words in alphabetical order as reinforcement of dictionary skills. Some pupils will need an alphabet line where letters are written across the top of the page to do this successfully.

Creative activities might include: role play, making menus on the word processor using clip art and borders, a design an exotic pizza competition or running a French food stall for Comic Relief. There are examples of homework activities in Appendices 3.4 and 3.5.

Differentiation by support

We know that some students need more help than others to complete a given task. If we provide help we are also providing differentiation by support. The strategies suggested in this section provide guidance on how differentiation by support may be given more systematically. Pupils work in a variety of ways and bring different abilities and aptitudes to that work. One form of differentiation is to provide a variety of tasks that cover the main content area in order to cater for the needs of individuals in the class. Some pupils need more help than others to complete a task. It is necessary to consider:

- individual support from the teacher;
- small group tutoring;
- support from other adults and students;
- support from technology;
- support by allocating more time to the task (particularly for dyslexic pupils, who have a reduced working memory capacity and thus take longer to process text).

At its simplest, differentiation by support may come down to the discussions that you have with your students. Whilst support for individual students is a vital ingredient in differentiated teaching, do bear in mind the constraints:

- You can't teach each pupil separately.
- Some pupils don't like one-to-one conversations with the teacher.
- Pupils taught separately are not being included in the group.

Small group tutoring may be better. Here you work with a small group for part of the lesson. They are still interacting with other pupils and are learning ways of working without constant one-to-one attention. In some cases, the pupil needs support for some parts of the course but is able to work more independently at other times. Change the pace of the lesson to make sure that pupils understand the concept being presented. One of the things we often overlook in the classroom is that some pupils just need extra time to explore, create, question and experience as they learn.

Support from adults and other pupils

Sometimes support is needed for recording. Teachers often provide handouts for some of the pupils but rely on them to jot down homework, and then wonder why it does not get done. Perhaps TAs could be made available to assist at this point. Could a good note-taker be used in paired or group work? Could pupils sometimes use a digital recorder or video for reporting results, recording facts, keeping notes, telling stories and so on? Could there be electronic versions of worksheets? Is a clickable grid appropriate? Should it have words, phrases or symbols?

The role of the learning support assistant (LSA) will be covered in Chapter 5. At the very least, an LSA can provide a very welcome extra pair of hands and a listening ear. At best, they provide expertise in matching a task to the individual student. However, it is very important that the teacher monitors this and does not abdicate responsibility for that particular student.

Support from technology

Technology can be used to present information, to help interpret it and to increase student independence in recording work. The following are excellent ways of linking picture and word:

- Get pictures from the 'Royalty-free clip art collection for foreign/second language instruction' at www.sla.purdue.edu/fll/japanproj/flclipart/.

Quand il neige, je porte un bonnet et une écharpe.

Figure 3.11 Using images to illustrate vocabulary
© Storybird

- Use a word-processing package with pictures or symbols, such as Clicker.
- Use 'Writing with symbols' or 'Inclusive writer'.
- Clip art can be used to illustrate ideas or vocabulary.
- Images and digital videos are stimulating (see Figure 3.11).

Pupils learn to link the written and spoken word and seem to learn vocabulary and structures much faster this way. The following are suggestions of ways in which you can capitalise on this fact:

- Ivona.com has the facility for pupils to type in their own short text and have it read aloud by authentic male or female voices in a wide variety of languages.
- An app such as Duolingo enables pupils to hear words as they construct sentences and has a variety of exercise types of different levels of challenge, from simple word recognition to translation into the target language.
- If text is in an electronic form it can be read by a talking word processor, printed out in Braille, made huge, or split up into manageable chunks.
- In a game from Textivate.com, answering questions correctly passes the ball to another player on your team. Consecutive correct answers will eventually score a goal.

Word-processing packages have many uses:

- Word processing can support those pupils with literacy problems who write very slowly and find it difficult to form letters.
- A word-processing package helps teachers present their work more effectively, making it easy for the teacher to adapt a basic worksheet to simplify or amplify it.
- Use a word processor for cloze exercises, drag and drop or sentence reordering, using colour to highlight past tenses.
- Spreadsheets are a good way to revisit food vocabulary and cost a meal or a party.
- Databases can be used for personal description or hobbies. 'Junior viewpoint' from Logotron might be a good place to start work on data handling.

Other recommended software packages include:

- Text manipulation software which can be used to revisit grammatical structures.
- Drill and practise programs which cover grammatical points. Some pupils benefit from focusing on a narrow subset of skills, such as forming past participles, until they are well internalised and they can use them without thinking. Other pupils work through this sort of program very fast but no learning takes place because they are not able to transfer their skills to other contexts.

- Mind-mapping software, such as Popplet or Bubbl.us can help build up letters and documents on the board as a whole class activity.
- Presentation software such as PowerPoint, Prezi, PowToon or Glogster or apps such as ExplainEverything or ShowMe can be a really visual way to introduce new vocabulary or explain grammar points.

Some final suggestions:

- Websites in the authentic target language can motivate students by making language learning seem real. For example, Mamalisa is a very good source of authentic children's songs and rhymes.
- Web-based interactive games using authoring software such as Quia, Hot Potatoes, Zondle are an enjoyable way of learning.
- Email can be a fun way of linking your class to a school abroad or even to a school in another part of Britain. An organisation like eTwinning can take a lot of the strain out of the process by linking you with a school in the country whose language you are studying. There is also the British Council Global Classrooms project.

Differentiation by response

In the 'old days', teachers usually had one set of responses to pupils – a grade and a written comment. This still has its place – in fact we are often encouraged to give marks and to match pupils' achievement to a set of criteria or statements. But this may not be particularly meaningful to the pupils themselves. We need to consider how we record and evaluate work and find ways of exploiting:

- individual action plans;
- pairs and group work;
- learning logs.

What are we working on?

It is important that students know what they have to do. This may sound obvious but most teachers just tell pupils. What happens if they are not listening at that moment? What happens if they are absent? So often pupils only have a hazy idea of what they are working on. They can remember what happened in class last week: 'We did a bit about rivers, animals on a farm, and "camping" is the same word in English and French, and Billy Moffat got sent out for throwing things.' That is a far cry from knowing that they are working on structures and vocabulary for holidays!

A simple way to keep track of the curriculum and objectives is to write them down on a piece of paper and pin them up somewhere in the MFL area.

A noticeboard could be developed with separate sections for different year groups. Keep referring to it till the objectives are fulfilled. It can be written in pupil friendly language, and have symbols or pictures. If we want to help pupils make real progress and become more independent, we have to share the aims with learners, so they will know what they are aiming for and when they have achieved it. Of course this does not have to be in print – it could be done in symbols, with pictures, or in Braille.

Pair work

Languages are about communication and talking, so why do many schools spend so much time making everyone do their piece of work quietly and on their own? If ever a subject was made for collaborative pair work, it is language learning. Everyone will have talents – from the child with a good memory who can recall a word others have forgotten, to the child with good dictionary skills who can look up words, to the child who can mimic well and has a limited vocabulary but a good sense of how the language should sound.

Sharing ideas and putting thoughts into words helps students learn (see Figure 3.12). Often it engages problem-solving skills instead of just dealing with, and repeating, received information. If we don't know how to say something in a foreign language we have to develop strategies to get round the problem.

Figure 3.12 Putting thoughts into words
© Foxlane Photos

These might involve asking someone else, looking it up, or finding things we do know and working out if we can adapt those. These are all real-life strategies which will stand pupils in good stead when they go abroad.

Providing learning logs

There is a fashion now for pupils to record their feelings and evaluate their own learning. Is it worth it? If a pupil just writes 'OK' every time, are we any further forward? Does it serve any purpose other than to add to a mound of paperwork? Some schools work with a line, as shown in Figure 3.13.

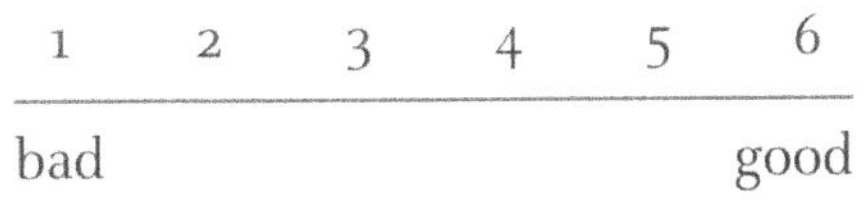

1	2	3	4	5	6
bad					good

Figure 3.13 Learning line

Pupils circle the number which comes closest to their views. Always have six choices rather than five, otherwise everyone circles number 3! Other schools use words or symbols to speed up the process.

Think about pupils doing this recording and evaluating in pairs. They will need to be taught the rudiments of peer assessment so that they can offer constructive criticism. This is sometimes referred to as 'FISH' feedback – it is **F**riendly, **I**nformative, **S**pecific and **H**elpful. The work of Professor John Hattie is very useful in this regard. Quality feedback that pupils subsequently act upon plays a significant role in helping them to improve (see www.youtube.com/watch?v=S770g-LULFY). This aspect will be explored in greater depth in Chapter 4. Pupils may think they have done really badly, but someone else may be able to say, 'Well, the first bit was good when we did about the weather, but then we didn't know any words for sports.' A conversation like this is a far more valuable evaluation than all the bits of paper!

Note

1 Query on Inclusion website: http://inclusion.ngfl.gov.uk

4 Monitoring and assessment

Why assess?

This may seem a strange question when we work in an era that sometimes seems to be obsessed with measuring pupil competency and pupil progress. Some people argue that assessments are just tests which show what children can't do. They say targets are imposed solely by staff or external bodies to provide standardised scores for league tables. They feel that such assessments generate figures that give no real indication of whether pupils are working to their full potential, and may disadvantage pupils with special needs. However, if we are just going through the motions and seeing assessment as an administrative requirement, we are missing the point.

At a simple level, assessment should check whether pupils have completed work. MFL teachers will need to record progress in all four skill areas (reading, writing, speaking and listening) over a period of time. Regular marking and recording enables teachers to see which units pupils have missed. Although language learning is not linear, pupils often need to acquire one set of skills in order to move on to the next level. Where children have missed a lesson where a grammar point was explained, they may have an incomplete understanding of how the language works. Assessment can point up the gaps in their reasoning.

Assessment provides an ideal opportunity to check whether learning has taken place, to test out the success of teaching methods and to tailor provision to meet the needs of individual pupils. Monitoring and assessment should give not just a set of grades but also promote reflection about what works, which styles of learning predominate in a group and how to remediate or extend limited knowledge. We also need to consider the pupil's own place in the process in terms of self-assessment.

Departmental handbooks are an important starting point for establishing clear procedures and guidance for MFL teachers on assessment matters. The most effective handbooks link assessment, recording and reporting policy for MFL to objectives in the departmental development plan, with analysis of assessment data contributing to annual action plans and directly influencing medium- and long-term planning. For example, teachers use information about pupils' specific strengths and weaknesses well in planning future units and lessons, such as in targeting weak areas of vocabulary or deficiencies in spelling.

As far as Ofsted is concerned, the following statement in the document *National curriculum and assessment from September 2014: Information for schools* sets out that organisation's expectations:

> Ofsted do not have any predetermined view as to what specific assessment system a school should use. Inspectors' main interest will be whether the approach adopted by a school is effective. They will be looking to see that it provides accurate information showing the progress pupils are making. The information should be meaningful for pupils, parents and governors. Ofsted recently wrote to all schools informing them how inspection in 2014/15 and beyond will take account of the removal of national curriculum levels.
>
> (DfE 2014: 4)

Further guidance may be obtained by studying the work of the Assessment Innovation Fund schools, which were:

> Durrington High School, West Sussex
> Frank Wise School, Banbury
> Hillyfield Primary Academy, Walthamstow
> Sirius Academy, Hull
> Swiss Cottage School, Camden
> Trinity Academy, Halifax
> Westminster Academy, London
> West Exe Technology College, Exeter.

(See www.gov.uk/government/news/schools-win-funds-to-develop-and-share-new-ways-of-assessing-pupils)

Formative assessment

When teachers and LSAs start working with a new group, it is important to assess prior knowledge. While reports may be passed on from the previous year, they can be unreliable guides. Some pupils make enormous leaps in their development over the school holidays, while others seem to forget everything they have been taught. It is a good idea to have a settling-in period of a few lessons to recall the language and to practise all four skills before any more formal assessment takes place. Without an assessment, staff, pupils and TAs may have no clear idea of what the pupils can and can't do or of the best ways of helping them to learn. Formative assessment can:

- provide a diagnostic tool;
- help staff to identify misconceptions and misunderstandings;
- highlight underachievement;
- support target-setting and/or monitoring;
- help teachers to clarify objectives;
- help with future planning;
- help teachers to anticipate future problems;
- help teachers to develop appropriate challenge;
- let the pupil see what they *can* do;
- raise expectations – for both staff and pupils.

In many ways, the assessment process is cyclical. For example, during a listening comprehension activity about daily routines, the teacher will check that all pupils understand how to express the time in the target language and indeed that they can all tell the time. If problems are identified, the teacher could decide to use warm-up activities on numbers, time and the 24-hour clock at the beginning of the next lesson. In other words, formative assessment needs to inform planning.

There is a wealth of detailed information about formative assessment in languages in the small booklet *Modern foreign languages inside the black box* (Jones and Wiliam 2008).

Finding out what works and what doesn't

Assessment is not just about remediation or plugging the gaps. Sometimes teachers don't realise that assessment is about their successes and failures too. 'I've taught them about the imperfect and how to use it but hardly any of them got it right in their homework' translates into 'I've told them but they haven't learnt it.' The wise teacher thinks, 'There must be another way', and sets about finding it. It may be that the imperfect was explained in a way that only worked for the good listeners, and she needs to make adjustments for those who operate on a more visual level. Sometimes using an electronic demonstration on a whiteboard can help those pupils who need extra practice on some features of the target language. Animations and sound effects can bring a topic to life and make it more memorable. The important point here is that when assessment throws up gaps in knowledge across a significant number of pupils, the teacher needs to reconsider strategies.

Teachers need to think about how they use questioning. Is it to improve pronunciation or to check on knowledge of grammar and vocabulary? How might they elicit longer answers? Typical questions which would do so could be pinned on the wall, with examples of short, medium and long answers, e.g.:

Quel temps fait-il?
Il neige.   Il neige et il fait froid.   Il neige, il fait froid et le ciel est noir.

Je peux vous aider?

Je voudrais une chambre.

Je voudrais une chambre pour deux personnes.

Je voudrais une chambre pour deux personnes pour trois nuits, du lundi au jeudi.

Alternatively, give pupils a grid:

Je voudrais une chambre		
pour . . . nuits	*avec*	*y-a-t'il . . . ?*
du ... au	un grand lit douche salle du bain bidet chauffage central balcon vue sur mer	un court de tennis un solarium un jardin une piscine un restaurant

Homework is crucial as it gives pupils time and space to practise and extend their learning as well as providing evidence of achievement. It needs to be followed up in class and seen as an integral part of the learning process and not just as an optional extra. However, the teacher does not necessarily need to see each piece of homework: pupils can mark each other's work in class with appropriate guidance and will often be far tougher on one another than the teacher would be.

You might find that a particular teaching strategy results in exceptionally good learning. Once you find out what works with particular pupils, you can think about how to extend the same methods to other topics. You may need to differentiate assessments. You can test the same points at different levels or in different ways. For an example of this when testing German vocabulary, see Appendix 3.5.

Of course, external examinations come in a prescribed form but you may find that you can better gauge what pupils can do at the end of a unit by devising creative assessments which link more closely to the ways they access and process knowledge. Role play, pupil-generated quizzes and dialogues may be effective tests of knowledge and understanding.

Ongoing formal assessment

The original national curriculum guidance was a good starting point for thinking about assessment. It stated that assessment approaches used by teachers are appropriate if they:

- ensure that pupils are given the chance and encouragement to demonstrate their competence and attainment through appropriate means;
- are familiar to the pupils and for which they have been adequately prepared;
- use materials which are free from discrimination and stereotyping in any form;
- provide clear and unambiguous feedback to pupils to aid further learning.

In order to overcome potential barriers to learning and assessment for individuals and groups of pupils, teachers should set targets for learning that:

- build on pupils' knowledge, experiences, interests and strengths to improve areas of weakness and demonstrate progression over time;
- are attainable and yet challenging and help pupils to develop their self-esteem and confidence in their ability to learn.

P levels

These are for pupils who are working at lower levels of achievement, and offer a useful way of monitoring progression.

P4 Pupils attempt to repeat, copy or imitate some sounds heard in the target language. They may perform familiar or simple actions on request, using repetition, sign or gesture as prompts. They listen and may respond to familiar rhymes and songs in a foreign language.

P5 Pupils attempt one or two words in the target language in response to cues in a song or familiar phrase. They respond to simple questions, requests or instructions about familiar events or experiences. Responses may be through vocalisation, sign or gesture, and pupils' responses may depend upon repetition and support.

P6 Pupils respond to others in a group. Their attempts to communicate in the target language may rely heavily upon repetition and gesture, and they may use facial expression and/or intonation to enhance meaning. They communicate positives and negatives in the target language in response to simple questions. They match and select symbols for familiar words, actions or objects presented in the target language.

P7 Pupils introduce themselves by name in response to a question in the target language. They contribute to using the target language for a purpose, for example using ICT skills to access the Internet and exchange information, with guidance from other pupils or adults. They listen, attend to and follow familiar interactions in the target language.

P8 Pupils listen attentively and know that the target language conveys meaning. They understand one or two simple classroom commands in the target language. They respond briefly using single words, signs or symbols. They may need considerable support from a spoken model and from visual clues. They may read and understand a few words presented in a familiar context with visual clues. They can copy out a few words with support. They label one or two objects. With some support, they use the target language for a purpose, for example requesting items in simulations of real life encounters in the target language.

Life after levels

One issue following on from the abolition of levels is that of comparability. If everyone is developing their own assessment systems in isolation, how can there be comparability? A reasonable *point de départ* might be the European Common Framework of Reference (ECFR), elaborated by the Council of Europe (www.coe.int/t/dg4/linguistic/Source/Framework_EN.pdf). This would at least give a common terminology for the discussion. There has also been some interesting work done by Rachel Hawkes, Director of International Education and Research at Comberton Academy Trust. She has developed a ten step assessment framework, drawing on both the ECFR and the Language Ladder (www.rachelhawkes.com/PandT/Assessment_2015/Assess2015.php).

The Professional Development Consortium in Modern Foreign Languages (PDC in MFL) has elaborated eight principles for successful language learning (https://pdcinmfl.files.wordpress.com/2013/03/8-principles-of-teaching-and-learning-in-mfl.pdf) which link through into their alternative assessment framework for modern languages (https://pdcinmfl.files.wordpress.com/2013/07/assessment-framework-for-mfl-april-13.pdf). The framework is divided into five levels: beginner, experimenter, developing, competent and skilled. Each of these levels is sub-divided into two broad areas: 'Just meeting this level' and 'Comfortably meeting this level', based on clear descriptors. So it should be possible to put together a framework which addresses the needs of SEND pupils, drawing on these two initiatives and maybe with a flavour of the P levels.

A more recent development is the initiative from Pearson Education, who have elaborated a 12-step progression scale covering KS3 up to GCSE. For ages 11–16, from KS3 to GCSE, they have created 12 steps representing low to high performance. There are descriptors to describe what a student on each step should be expected to do in each of the four skills and a grammar scale for reference.

They assume no prior knowledge from KS2 so the first step is indicative of an old NC level 1.

The expectation is for KS3 to span the first to the seventh or eighth steps with some pupils achieving fewer steps and some achieving more.

(See www.pearsonschoolsandfecolleges.co.uk/AssetsLibrary/SECTORS/ Secondary/SUBJECT/Support-for-Progression/Introduction-to-11-16- Progression-Support-from-Pearson-MFL-Version for the steps and more.)

Ongoing informal assessment

Not all assessment has to be in the form of a test. Some teachers use focused observation. This gives them a chance to evaluate strengths and weaknesses. If the class is working in small groups, it is an ideal time to check out such matters as turn taking, who is silent, who lacks concentration, who opts out, which pupils perform better in groups rather than whole-class situations, who has a good accent, who needs help with pronunciation, whether there are any signs of bullying, etc. It may also be a good time to check on particular points on support plans. If a pupil is working on listening skills or behavioural targets, these can be observed too.

Cloze is a good way of assessing whether learning has taken place. Often it is hard to establish what pupils know if they have problems with speaking or writing. A cloze passage enables them to fill in the gaps without getting bogged down in explanations or being held back by poor articulation or slow handwriting.

Several variations on the example in Figure 4.1 can be made using 'Mix & Gap' from Task Magic software, and completed by pupils on a computer or tablet.

son	es	más	sendero
día	típico	disfrutar	acceso
puede	duda	famoso	tomaremos

Primero, visitaremos la Plaza de España y _____ un aperitivo o cerveza en El Pintor Blanco, _____ bar. Luego cenaremos en un restaurante _____ estilo buffet antes de _____ un espectáculo de flamenco. En la misma zona, Estrillo _____ una aldea de pescadores, perfecta para un _____ de descanso. Sin _____ , las playas en esta parte _____ muy lindas! El _____ está a través de un _____ en el bosque. Playa Nima es la playa _____ próxima del Centro donde se _____ bañar.

Figure 4.1 Cloze passage to check understanding of Spanish

Feedback to pupils

Apart from question and answer activities in class, marking is the most obvious form of feedback. Drill and practice computer programs are particularly effective in this context because they provide speedy individualised responses in a way that a teacher in a class of 30 pupils cannot. They can check a response, urge a pupil to try again if they have chosen an incorrect answer, provide explanations and offer rewards in the form of sound effects, animations or even printed certificates on successful completion of tasks. However, they only work well for certain forms of learning and for developing particular skills. They can help with grammar, vocabulary and spelling where accuracy is paramount but they are not suitable for more creative tasks. Drill and practice software is good for motivating some pupils and has a lot to offer to learners who have a short attention span or who need considerable over-learning in order to retain particular structures.

Drill and practice activities are a good form of testing and the better programs keep a record of pupil responses so teachers can see how many attempts a pupil made before getting a right answer. In practice, this information is sometimes so detailed that a teacher needs a considerable amount of time to track each pupil.

Teacher marking needs to be prompt and in a form that the pupils can understand. Although it is good to put comments in the target language, some pupils working at P levels would not understand the difference between *très bien* and *assez bien*. A system of different coloured stickers may make the point more effectively. Some teachers like to divide marks to record effort and result so pupils see that it is worth trying harder and that this will be rewarded, but pupils need a clear understanding of the difference between effort and attainment.

Marking should be as detailed as possible. The teacher needs to pick out errors and show how to improve accuracy (e.g. position of adjectives, gender, use of capitals/lower case, etc.). Pupils need to be set targets and shown what they need to do to improve. The teacher also needs to provide oral feedback to the individual and/or to the class, making teaching points out of the more common mistakes. This is for the benefit of those who do not necessarily obtain information from text.

Pupils know what to do

Effective assessment involves constant monitoring and feedback to pupils and appropriate action to promote improvement, as in the following example:

> The teacher picks up points to correct in plenary, and does so rigorously and sensitively, getting the class to repeat the correct answers so that all can benefit without individual pupils being demoralised. She gives credit for an 'almost right' answer, but doesn't stop there. She commends pupils who take the initiative in going beyond the minimum with an extended utterance, in order to raise the expectations of the rest. In monitoring oral work in pairs, she explains how the utterance can be improved, using reference to similar patterns or to work covered earlier.
>
> (Ofsted 2003)

Pupils tend to find it easier to identify their progress in written than in oral work, but oral work does have one advantage in that it offers the possibility of quick feedback. In general, their awareness of how well they are doing is linked to the amount of effort invested by teachers into explaining criteria and systems. For example, in the report quoted above, Ofsted commented:

> Pupils were made well aware of how they were doing in speaking during 'routine' oral work, and by periodic mini-tests in speaking, which they had to re-do until they got a satisfactory mark. They were alerted to the most common errors in writing as these were discussed by the teachers with the whole class. In another school, pupils could explain what was expected in terms of the school's content–language accuracy mark scheme and were provided with very clear information about effort grades, homework marking, and examination criteria.

Tell them, show them, work with them so they have a clear idea of what sort of work they should produce. Again, be explicit. For example:

Tu es en vacances avec ta famille. Écris une carte postale (environ 30 mots) à ton correspondant canadien/ta correspondante canadienne.

Où es-tu? (la ville ou la région)
Que fais-tu? (du sport? des visites? etc.)
Quel temps fait-il? (froid? beau? etc.)
Quand tu rentres en Angleterre?

Pupils need to know exactly what is required:

- I want you to write between 25 and 40 words.
- You must put something for each of the questions.
- There must be a greeting such as *Salut*.
- There must be a goodbye phrase such as *A bientôt* to show you have finished.
- You must sign it.

They might also need a model to adapt. Modelling is a powerful way of demonstrating to pupils exactly what is required of them. Many teachers use the 'WAGOLL' approach: **W**hat **A** **G**ood **O**ne **L**ooks **L**ike. This can lead to a discussion of the elements that make this model a good piece of work and helps pupils internalise the criteria. It is also a significant step towards developing peer assessment, as pupils begin to identify the positive elements that the work possesses, and the elements which might be missing or improved upon.

So, if a pupil's answer is not quite right, you could talk to them about it but they might not take it in. You could ask them to do it again but it might be no better. Instead, find a pupil's work which is that little bit better than theirs and get them to tell you where the difference lies. It might be an idea to photocopy some of the strongest responses for use in this way (possibly erasing the pupil's name). An answer might be, for example, 'She put more about what they did on holiday.' If you show pupils the best work in the class, it is too far ahead of where the less able pupils are so they will switch off. Find work which is the next stage up from theirs. It also gives a boost to the child whose work is chosen. Work together with the child or pair them up with another pupil to bring their work up a notch. Self-assessment plays an important role in helping pupils to understand assessment objectives and criteria.

In effective MFL departments, recording and analysis of assessment information are complemented by focused target setting. Targets are included in reports and discussed during parent/pupil interviews. An Ofsted report, for example, states:

GCSE grades are estimated at three points in Key Stage 4: December of Year 10, end of Year 10, after Year 11 mocks. On each occasion these are shared and discussed with pupils in 'off timetable' individual interviews. Another school sets interim learning targets, such as 'learn the spelling of these ten words' as opposed to 'improve your spelling' which is too general. Each pupil has a summary sheet on which he/she must enter 'what I have done about this'. The teacher signs off each target when it is achieved.

(Ofsted 2003)

Individual support plans

One secondary school has developed a modular curriculum across Key Stage 3. All modules run for half a term and have their own course booklet stating the overall aims, as well as containing some of the learning resources, activities and evaluation materials. They then have a menu of objectives, perhaps a dozen. During the first lesson of the new half term in each subject, pupils negotiate with the teacher, identifying five or six appropriate targets from the list, for example:

Je dois appendre:

les jours	les sports
les mois	les nombres jusqu' à vingt
les passetemps	les animaux

Each pupil has a personal organiser and these targets are recorded so that they can be shared with parents and referred to both at school and when doing homework. Pupils, parents and teachers are delighted with the system, and are finding that even the youngest pupils are taking much more responsibility for their learning and taking a pride in their achievements. It has also helped tremendously with individual learning plans for pupils with special educational needs where the vast majority of the paperwork is now neatly contained in the pupils' personal organiser and teachers' regular class records, in just the same format as everyone else's. In a sense it means that for French, everyone has a support plan instead of just 'special' pupils.

A school in Nottingham has Bull's Eye sheets. Pupils write three targets they want to achieve: learn to count to 50, learn words for rooms in the house, learn how to say what I would like to eat. They work out how this will happen. Will they record the numbers digitally, will they sing them, recite them to a friend or their dad? How many numbers will they know by next week? How many the week after? The whole point is that they set the goals and work out how they will know if they are getting there.

External examinations

Pupils need practice in taking examinations. The first step, however, is to identify which examination is appropriate. If you are teaching modern foreign languages to students who are low achievers, or you need some kind of award to mark progress in French, Spanish or German, finding alternatives to GCSE has been made more difficult with the introduction of the English Baccalaureate, or EBacc. This requires pupils to sit GCSE examinations in English, maths, a science, a humanity and a foreign language, for which they will receive an additional endorsement on their certificates. It is a significant measure in performance tables and has therefore influenced option offers in many schools. Until the introduction of the EBacc there were several accreditation routes which were possibly more appropriate for low attaining pupils and those with special needs. Unfortunately these developments were effectively killed off by the insistence on the part of the government of the time that all pupils take GCSE examinations, and no equivalent qualifications. This 'one size fits all' approach has caused concern in the language teaching community that pupils with special needs are being effectively disenfranchised from languages by an assessment régime that does not meet their needs. This is compounded by the removal of the ability to mix and match tiers in the examination. Pupils must be entered either for Foundation or Higher in all papers. In addition, the high stakes nature of the league tables has the net effect that special needs pupils are sometimes 'encouraged' to look somewhere other than languages for their qualifications. Choice has been further eroded by the decision of OCR to withdraw from offering examinations in modern foreign languages as a result of delays in accrediting new specifications.

Accommodating the needs of pupils with SEN

As the examination approaches, you should think about whether special arrangements will be necessary for individual pupils. Examination boards are bound by legislation with regard to special educational needs (for example the Equality Act 2010), which means that candidates cannot be treated less favourably on the grounds of their disability in an exam setting. Exam boards are generally quite helpful about the special requirements for particular pupils to show their achievements.

The Joint Council for General Qualification issues guidance to exam boards and to centres (see www.jcq.org.uk/exams-office/access-arrangements-and-special-consideration/regulations-and-guidance/access-arrangements-and-reasonable-adjustments-2015-20). This guidance covers access arrangements, reasonable adjustments and special consideration. Copies of the guidance can be downloaded as .pdf documents from the site.

Schools need to ensure that:

- special assessment arrangements do not give unfair advantage over other candidates;
- arrangements are determined according to the particular disability or learning difficulty;
- users of certificates are not misled about candidate attainment.

The arrangements may include extra time, additional facilities or some level of support, for example pupils with a physical disability may be allowed a writer, extra time allowance (normally 25 per cent) and mechanical/electronic aids. Students with a visual impairment may have a writer, a reader, tapes, question papers with large print, Braille or Moon, use of a keyboard to produce typescript answers or raised type responses to a question paper, extra time allowance (normally 25 per cent) and mechanical/electronic equipment.

Awarding bodies will not provide enlarged question papers for candidates with such difficulties, but centres may, with the permission of the awarding body, open question papers up to one hour prior to the examination in order to make enlargements or photocopy onto coloured paper. Centres must take responsibility for ensuring that the entire paper is copied and for maintaining the security of the question paper.

Arrangements for pupils with a hearing impairment may include the use of a communicator/interpreter, extra time allowance (normally 25 per cent) and mechanical/electronic aids. Signing of questions or the oral presentation of questions using the oral/aural approach may be permitted for candidates with a hearing impairment (except where reading is an assessment objective) in exceptional circumstances, if either approach is the usual method of communication in the classroom and access to the examination cannot be achieved by other means. Special amplification for aural tests may be permitted for hearing-impaired candidates. Reading of the tests to enable candidates to lip-read may also be permitted. In addition, candidates whose hearing loss results in a possible linguistic disability may be provided with question papers with appropriate modified wording, as recommended by a specialist teacher of the deaf.

In the case of candidates with specific learning difficulties of a dyslexic or similar nature, arrangements may include a writer and/or a reader, extra time allowance (normally 25 per cent), tapes and typescripts of answers, and coloured overlays/paper. Some visual difficulties are normally corrected by the use of tinted spectacles or coloured overlays, and permission for the use of these aids does not have to be sought from the awarding body. Arrangements for candidates with other learning difficulties may include a writer and/or a reader, extra time allowance (normally 25 per cent) and other audio/visual aids as appropriate to the needs of the individual.

5 Managing support

At the time of writing, support staff numbers stand at 251,000 (full-time equivalent) in the 23,000 schools in England (DfE 2015b).

All teaching assistants, whether they are foreign language assistants or are employed to help pupils with special needs, need to be managed well and their role must be clear. This chapter will look at their work in relation to:

- helping with the care and support of individual pupils;
- helping with the care and support of a group of pupils;
- supporting learning activities;
- assisting with classroom resources and records.

Compare these scenarios:

Tom is a learning assistant in a Year 8 German class. He supports Malik, who has retinitis pigmentosa and has very little peripheral vision. Tom does not speak German. He and Malik sit at the back of the class and, when the German class is engaged in reading and writing activities, Tom spends the time testing Malik on his spellings for English or helping him catch up with his homework for other subjects.

Kuldip has severe learning difficulties. He is in Year 7, finds it hard to cope with the changes of lessons and is reluctant to speak in class. Myra, his TA, has collected some items for his German box. This contains a picture book about Germany, a small map, a picture of the Bayern Munich football team and an mp3 player with a recording of German greetings. She opens the box at the start of the lesson to help him get oriented. He sees the objects and it helps him to focus on German and call to mind

(Continued)

some of the words he knows so he has a context for learning. The class is working on *Zu Hause*. Although Myra has only been learning German alongside the class, she has copied some core vocabulary and structures from the worksheets onto a Clicker grid so Kuldip can build up a piece of writing and print it.

Alison has a good relationship with Billy, who has learning difficulties and some behavioural problems. She takes a keen interest in his welfare and if he is unhappy, he often seeks her out at lunchtime in the Base. She has made a real difference to his confidence but she is over-protective. She often praises him when he has made very little effort. There are also issues about how much of the work is his. The final straw was when the children had to draw their bedroom and then label the furniture in German for homework. Billy's work was really good, especially considering he was absent!

This latter scenario is typical of the 'helicopter' assistant, who hovers above the student until she makes a mistake and then swoops in to correct it for her.

What does an assistant do?

Support staff may be called by different names in different authorities. They may be called teaching assistants (TAs), special support assistants, pupil assistants, statement support assistants or learning support assistants (LSAs). Their role is to help teachers and to work with other professionals such as speech and language therapists and parents to support children's learning. Some are allocated to an individual pupil with special needs, while others support a whole class or groups within the class. Support staff may also provide administrative support, technical support or be involved in pastoral care.

While TAs do not 'teach', their input is crucial to successful teaching, and their observations inform the short- and long-term planning for individuals and whole classes. Sometimes teachers and TAs work together with experts, for example with advisory teachers, educational psychologists or speech and language therapists, to plan programmes for the pupil. Targets from these programmes can be incorporated into support plans.

There have been particularly lively discussions on Senco-forum about the variety of ways in which ancillary staff were used in schools. One school has two different categories of TA:

- Some TAs are used for general classroom support and are involved in:

  - photocopying;
  - displays;
  - helping with administration;
  - collecting money;
  - first aid (those who have done the training);
  - playground supervision;
  - being 'an extra adult' in the classroom to support as and when needed (often working with the least able or the most able to supervise differentiated group work).

- Other TAs, specifically attached to pupils who have special needs (as statemented provision)

  - work one-to-one or support a small group which includes that child;
  - help with preparation of materials;
  - support organisation and inclusion strategies;
  - deal with specific physio, speech and language or dyspraxia programmes and support plan targets;
  - carry out observations and keep records of progress.

Other schools have different models:

> We have SEND TAs, one for each year group, who support individual children and groups. We also have one general TA per class who supports children, but also does lots of organisational stuff (tidying, pencil sharpening and photocopying etc.). We always write these types of things into the job description, because somebody has to do it or the class/group doesn't function. Usually TA and teacher share tasks. (Senco-forum)

Helping with the care and support of individual pupils

Undoubtedly, some of the pupils would not access the curriculum or make the progress that they do without the expertise and encouragement that is provided by TAs. The TA will perform a variety of roles including acting as a scribe, simplifying instructions, providing key words, in the case of visual impairment making sure text is enlarged, and in all cases helping the pupil to achieve the targets in the support plan.

There are various ways of providing individualised support. The TA is in an ideal position to bolster up the pupil in a way that the class teacher does not have time to do. Ideally, the TA should:

- take an interest in the pupil's interests;
- notice when he or she is feeling low;
- give support when needed;
- encourage effort;
- develop listening skills;
- inspire confidence and trust;
- have positive expectations.

One of the central questions is: should TAs only work with the designated child? The answer to this will usually be 'no'. Some children with special needs don't like being singled out as the one needing extra help and sometimes the TA can effectively exclude the pupil as in the following example:

> Nuala has severe hearing loss. Her local authority has recently provided an audio typist to sit at her side and type what is said in class. Nuala reads this off a screen and so keeps pace with the rest of the group. However, this means that Nuala cannot choose where she sits in class or who she sits next to. She is welded to her typist. This is her main form of communication with the class. While everyone is looking and listening, her eyes are fixed on the screen and she misses a lot of the interaction. The school needs to reassess what her needs are and find a way of integrating her more fully in the class and meeting her communication needs.

This is typical of the 'Velcro' assistant; almost permanently attached to the student regardless of need or circumstance. I once observed a Year 8 French class in which there were 12 students and 7 adults: teacher, FLA and 5 TAs, each 'Velcroed' to a statemented student. Happily this has changed for the better as many schools now do a budget of TA hours rather than simply allocate a body to each student. With the advent of the Pupil Premium and increased scrutiny on how the funding is disbursed and utilised, schools have recognised that it is important to maximise the effectiveness of TAs for the greater number of pupils, as opposed to the older, more labour-intensive model which was less effective.

Indeed, the Education Endowment Foundation's TA Guidance Report of 2014 highlighted the dangers of using support staff in an informal and unstructured manner:

> Those pupils receiving the most support from TAs made less progress than similar pupils who received little or no support from TAs. There was also evidence that the negative impact was most marked for pupils with the highest levels of SEN, who, as discussed, typically receive the most TA support.
> (https://v1.educationendowmentfoundation.org.uk/
> uploads/pdf/TA_Guidance_Report_Interactive.pdf)

This report also makes reference to other studies, notably the Deployment and Impact of Support Staff (DISS) Project Report of 2008 (see below), and further concludes:

> The DISS study was completed in 2008. Although there is no exact comparison available, experience and evidence gained during the more recent Effective Deployment of Teaching Assistants (EDTA) and Making a Statement (MAST) studies, conducted between 2010 and 2013, suggests the use of TAs has not changed substantially since then.

There is some good news, however, as the report states:

> there is emerging evidence that TAs can provide noticeable improvements to pupil attainment. Here, TAs are working well alongside teachers in providing excellent complementary learning support, although, importantly, this is happening in a minority of classrooms and schools.

This minority of schools have presumably taken on board the lessons of time budgeting and enhancing the wider pedagogical role of support staff, as well as providing greater access for SEND pupils to the subject specialist teacher. This may well be one way of avoiding the caveat with regard to pupil behaviour, motivation and approaches to learning mentioned in the report: 'There is mixed evidence to support the view that TA support has a positive impact on "soft" outcomes. Some evidence suggests TA support may increase dependency.' In terms of impact on learning outcomes, the report refers to another potential issue in one of its key findings: 'TAs tend to be more concerned with task completion and less concerned with developing understanding.' This aspect is further explored in more detail in the report:

> Evidence from classroom recordings made during the DISS project revealed that the quality of instruction pupils received from TAs was markedly lower compared to that provided by the teacher. TAs tended to close talk down and 'spoon-feed' answers [14,15]. Over time, this can limit understanding, weaken pupils' sense of control over their learning and reduce their capacity to develop independent learning skills.

This is not to say, however, that support staff must never be used in small group or one-to-one interventions. The proviso is that such interventions are structured and the staff have access to high quality support and training:

> The area of research showing the strongest evidence for TAs having a positive impact on pupil attainment focuses on their role in delivering structured interventions in one-to-one or small group settings. This research shows a consistent impact on attainment of approximately three to four additional

months' progress over an academic year (effect size 0.2–0.3) [1,29,30]. This can be seen as a moderate effect. Crucially, these positive effects are only observed when TAs work in structured settings with high-quality support and training. When TAs are used in more informal, unsupported instructional roles, we see little or no impact on pupil outcomes (see Section 3.1 What is the impact of TAs on pupils' academic attainment?) [2]. This suggests that schools should consider using well-structured interventions with reliable evidence of effectiveness.

Even in these days when the term 'inclusion' is quite widely understood, there is still a real danger of walking into a classroom and seeing a child with Down's syndrome or a pupil with a visual impairment sitting in a different part of the room doing different tasks. This cannot be justified as differentiation!

There is also an issue about making the best use of the TA's time. What if the class is watching a video? Does the TA need to be there? What if they are engaged in pair work? Does three become a crowd? What if the child is ill, does the TA get paid? There are also issues of dependence. It is true that children needing specialist equipment get fed up with 'breaking in' new learning assistants and find it easier to work with someone who knows how the kit works and how best to help them. On the other hand, if that TA is ill or leaves, the child can feel bereft. One-to-one support is fraught with dangers. There is a school of thought which runs along these lines: 'Kerry's speech is hard to understand and she seems very happy working with Mel. Mel knows what she's doing so I let her get on with it. This gives me more time to work with others who need help.' In this case, Kerry might just as well be in another class.

You may want the TA to concentrate on one child but supplement this with keeping an eye on other children in the class who are falling behind or need extra stimulation. This can be tricky if the TA insists that the job description specifies supporting one individual. It might be worth pointing out that no child works in isolation and part of the TA's role is to ensure an inclusive setting which cannot be achieved by isolating the child and smothering him or her with one-to-one attention.

The teacher's role is to teach and to make sure that there are activities which are within the grasp of all the pupils in the classroom. Where there is a good relationship with a TA planning does become a joint enterprise. The good TA is always aware that the individual is also part of a group and will do everything to foster good relations between pupils. Indeed, in the most effective working arrangements there is an almost seamless transition between TA and class teacher, which gives the class teacher time with the special needs students while the TA supervises the rest of the group. After all, don't the special needs students actually need the expertise of the subject specialist a bit more than the others?

Helping with the care and support of a group of pupils

Many TAs find they are supporting a group of low achievers, rather than one named child. Again there is a danger of dividing the class into subsets. Many of us have seen classrooms where there is an obvious 'remedial table'. If a group of the more challenging children are sitting together under the direction of the TA, they are being segregated, not included. This approach also sets up problems in the long term because children

* become dependent on the TA and will not get on with work if left unsupervised;
* develop irritating behavioural tics learnt from each other through peer modelling;
* have low self-esteem because they are in the 'thickies group';
* fail to benefit from working with pupils who have different strengths and weaknesses;
* receive too little direct teaching from the class teacher because the TA is in attendance;
* are not set sufficiently challenging tasks.

Working with groups of pupils means that there are obvious time savings but there may be a danger that the quieter pupils miss out because the louder ones demand attention. Guidelines for working with learners in the MFL classroom are given in Appendix 5.1.

It is more effective to pinpoint individuals who will benefit from extra support and to specify what that support might be. It is the teacher's job to decide how the lessons will proceed and what styles of teaching are appropriate. Where possible, the teacher should provide the TA with a lesson plan with notes about individual pupils. This can be very simple as in this example of a lesson, based on checking and reinforcing French town vocabulary:

Teacher	*Pupils*	*Notes to TA*
Hold up pictures.	Call out vocabulary.	Tom at front please.
Distribute scissors + vocabulary sheet	Cut up to make flash cards.	
Chez moi.		**Enlarged pictures for Tom.** Watch Louise with scissors. Shannon will need help cutting. Don't let Arun and Kyle sit together.

(Continued)

Check understanding, answer questions.	Draw pictures.	Check all five on task; get Shannon to draw at least four!

As well as working alongside the teacher in class, the TA may also withdraw pupils for some specialist support. They may work one-to-one: helping with problem solving, providing pastoral support, giving active listening or catching up with work. Alternatively, there may be small groups focusing on social skills, problem solving or anger management, and the timetabling for this should be negotiated between the SENCO and subject teachers.

Where teacher and TA are working together in a class, there needs to be a consistent approach. They need to share the same philosophy and agree classroom management:

> It took time for classroom culture to change to the extent that the second adult felt free to move around while the lead teacher was delivering the substance of the lesson. There were also potential tensions when adolescents inevitably tested the boundaries. It was important that the support teacher was able to sit calmly in the classroom and read unspoken signals from the lead teacher. Both teachers needed to have a will to make working together effective for the children, even if sometimes it meant hiding feelings and deferring to each other.
>
> (Lovey 2002: 7)

Supporting learning activities

Apart from specific care for individual pupils, TAs can provide general support for study skills. This might include:

- producing a visual timetable;
- checking that the pupil has the right equipment for lessons: pens, coloured pencils, rulers, dictionary, etc.;
- dealing with mounds of bits of paper which collect in the pupil's bag or folders and helping the pupil to be organised;
- providing extra practice for spellings;
- reinforcing key vocabulary;
- showing the pupil how to set out work neatly;
- keeping a check on homework, especially if the child is not going to get support at home;
- helping with structuring revision.

TAs may need to learn how particular resources help particular pupils. For instance, there are various MFL computer-assisted learning packages with exercises and listening practice and they may need to learn how to use these programs.

Sometimes, their role grows and expands to encompass a whole new approach as in this example:

Brakenhale is a community comprehensive school for 11–18 year olds. Of the 633 students, 46 per cent are on the school's special needs register and 17 have statements – over half these statements include emotional and behavioural difficulties and moderate learning difficulties. There is a high turnover of staff and the school has had particular difficulties with children with learning and behavioural problems.

TAs, however, are not given a hard time by the vast majority of pupils because they are seen as allies and friends. TAs are helpful negotiators with the pupils. According to the SENCO:

- We have evidence that the TAs do much good for the pupils.
- We can evidence improved attendance.
- We can show increases in reading age measures.
- The TAs can identify the pupils who are not coping, often better than teachers who have other concerns to address.
- The TAs have improved the social skills of youngsters.
- 'Sort and support' pupils show real improvement.

Often the TAs swap roles with teachers, with the TA managing the whole class while the teacher deals with individuals. The TAs also work with the newly established homework club and provide the total supervision for five nights per week.[1]

Assisting with classroom resources and records

TAs may be employed to assist with paperwork, filing and resource management, and consequently reduce teacher workloads. In the future, there is likely to be more administrative support in schools. The DfES circular 2/98 *Reducing the bureaucratic burden on teachers* (DfES 1999) listed 24 non-teaching tasks which teachers routinely perform and proposed that many of these should be undertaken by support staff so that teachers could focus more closely on teaching. Such tasks include:

- collecting money;
- chasing absences;
- bulk photocopying;
- copy typing;
- producing standard letters;
- producing class lists;
- record keeping and filing;
- making classroom displays;
- analysing attendance figures;
- processing exam results;
- collating pupil reports;
- administering work experience;
- administering examinations;
- administering teacher cover;
- ICT trouble shooting and minor repairs;
- commissioning new ICT equipment;
- ordering supplies and equipment;
- stocktaking;
- cataloguing, preparing, issuing and maintaining equipment and materials;
- minuting meetings;
- co-ordinating and submitting bids;
- seeking and giving personnel advice;
- managing pupil data;
- inputting pupil data.

Many of these tasks apply particularly to the MFL classroom. Teachers will welcome offers to help organise a trip to France, to collect money and make arrangements with the coach company etc., or to prepare letters to be sent home. The TA can work with staff and pupils to produce relevant lively wall displays, find out about new materials and programs, do stocktaking and cataloguing of books, worksheets, magazines, resources such as menus, games, etc. and in this way get to know more about the subject and how to tailor resources to pupils' needs.

As well as carrying out administrative tasks, the TA may generate additional classroom resources as in the following example:

> I used box filing cards, colour coded according to difficulty. When teaching mixed-ability groups for MFL, a box of cards was prepared for each module of the course. These were laminated so they could be taken home for homework. While giving out homework I knew by the colour at a glance which card to give. Each card was numbered so that there was a variety of activities at each level that would consolidate the learning according to the student's ability. If it was a listening exercise, the tape would have

a sticker of the same colour with the corresponding card number on it. The cards were often used in class and recording equipment was made available for students to record their sentences privately until they were satisfied.

(Lovey 2002: 54)

The child with a visual impairment will need additional resources and the RNIB offers this warning:

> When you are planning your classroom sessions, ensure that you liaise with the visually impaired child's support assistant or support teacher to advise them of any resources you intend to use. The amount of work needed to adapt resources into large print or Braille can be very time-consuming, particularly in language teaching, where many of the standard resources are very visual, with heavy reliance on cartoons, cursive script and busy pictures.
>
> So try not to change your mind at the last minute! If you are only likely to use two pages of a four-page worksheet, tell the support worker: they will appreciate not having to adapt those extra two pages! And give them ample time to produce resources in modified formats – it will be appreciated and will benefit you when your lessons are far more accessible for your pupil with sight problems![2]

Barriers to success

Communication is vital for harmonious working relationships in any department but there are particular issues within the MFL department. Many TAs do not speak a foreign language, or at least, have no confidence in their ability. While most support staff will happily have a go at history or maths or science, even though they are not experts in that area, they worry about their own skills in French or German. This can have a 'knock-on' effect. They may feel that they are no use and so arrange to support other children at that time in different classes. The 'I'm no good at languages' mentality may spread to the pupils who think, 'Well, if Mrs Clark can't do French, there's no point me trying.' In some schools, they get round this problem by allocating TAs to a particular subject or faculty but you are not necessarily going to find a TA who is good at several languages. However, one of the obvious strengths of using a TA who has no second language in the MFL department is that they see the lesson through the pupil's eyes. Invariably, this means that such a TA can provide useful feedback to the teacher.

MFL staff must ensure that the ethos of the department is obvious. TAs should be encouraged to take as active a role in languages as they would do in other subjects. Indeed, teachers should work hard to promote the notion that language classes are lively and fun. It is hard to engage and motivate staff who feel they are just carrying out 'dogsbody' duties or are just child-minding.

Different ways of allocating time

Schools have evolved different ways of using TA time. Sometimes the head of department is given a number of hours and has to decide how to use them most effectively to support the greatest number of pupils. In some schools, departments have to 'bid' for TA time; in others there are 'specialist' TAs for specific departments. Some schools use a different model and attach a group of TAs to a year group. The TAs come to know the children quite well as they support them in different areas of the curriculum and know something of their strengths and weaknesses, their preferred learning styles, what pressures they face and what triggers bad behaviour. They develop quite a close bond with the pupils and find strategies for encouraging them and keeping them on task. These qualities are more use to a class teacher than the ability to speak French.

Whatever model is used, it is worth noting that staffing tends to be more generous with departments who use TAs 'properly'. If the MFL department has a policy and can show that it uses TAs effectively and values them appropriately, they are more likely to receive a decent allocation of TA time. It is a good idea to consider some of the issues before term starts and discuss how the relationship between teacher and support staff will work. A review sheet is included as Appendix 5.1.

Support and guidance

Again, communication is the key to success. Ask the TAs what support and guidance they might need. Explain that if an activity seems to be pitched at the wrong level and the pupil is finding it too easy or too difficult, their role is to help in differentiation. This may mean:

- simplifying instructions, oral and written;
- adapting worksheets to make them easier to understand;
- presenting work in short 'chunks';
- providing key words;
- developing extension activities.

Remind them that their role is to find ways of increasing independence and allowing the pupils to show what they can do. It will not be necessary for them to work alongside a pupil at all times in all lessons; and under no circumstances should they do the work for a pupil. These might be their key duties and responsibilities:

- deal with equipment – specialist equipment and ICT;
- observe and record – the participation of individuals during group or class work;
- support group work – with objectives set by the teacher;
- support an individual – with care needs;
- support an individual – with a specific task set by the teacher;
- support an individual – with behavioural needs;
- administration – carry out administrative tasks set by the teacher;
- display – take charge of displaying work;
- training – attend relevant training sessions.

What if it goes wrong?

Sometimes, with the best will in the world, there is conflict between a teacher and the TA. You will find guidance in any number of management books about how to get the best from staff and deal with grievances but here are some strategies which have been used successfully in schools.

Deal with dissatisfaction *fast*. If a TA asks to speak to you, make time as soon as possible. Similarly, if you are unhappy about something, deal with it quickly. Things rarely improve if left unattended.

People may have legitimate grievances so it is important to listen and to keep an open mind. Listen to the content rather than the style of delivery and be aware that they may feel undervalued or unappreciated. Perhaps they have issues in their home life which are spilling over into the workplace, making them hard to deal with. You are not a counsellor. You can listen but you can only deal with the things which are in your power. You should not let yourself be caught up too much in personal issues.

Sometimes a very good TA can be a bit too motherly (this does apply to both sexes) and always knows best: 'Oh no, I don't think Lawrence would like that. He wouldn't be able to cope.' In some cases, the TA may be scared of stepping out of routine and trying something new; in other cases, they have a need to control everything which relates to 'their pupil'. This may be the time to talk to senior management about your fears that Lawrence is becoming too dependent and that it might be a good idea to foster a new relationship with another TA.

Here are some suggestions for dealing with more confrontational issues:

- Never discuss contentious issues in front of pupils. They gossip and exaggerate.
- Never say anything unpleasant about the TA. It could be slander but in any case it is unprofessional and sours working relationships.
- Remember, nothing in the workplace is really 'off the record'.
- Acknowledge that there is a problem. This can cut the confrontation down to size. By showing the other person that you recognise she is upset (even if the anger seems disproportionate), you are showing you take her seriously.
- Repeat back what has been said. When people hear their own words, they may be caught off guard by the reality of what they have said and may have to rethink it. You are also buying thinking time.
- Reword what the person has said: 'So, what you're really saying is . . . .' This causes her to reflect on the implications of what she has said or how she has said it.
- Summarise the discussion. When people are upset, they use a lot of words. Summarising means that you take out the rage and hurt and look at the real issue.
- Ask questions if you feel you are being dragged into an emotional minefield. For example, if a difficult person accuses you of something ludicrous, ask, in a non-threatening way, 'What are you trying to tell me?'
- Defer the discussion to another time in the near future if you cannot deal with it there and then or feel that emotion has overcome reason.
- If the conflict involves a third party, as it so often does, get them together in the same room. It is tempting to see them separately especially if tempers are frayed, but it is better if you can deal with it in an open forum so you cannot be accused of taking sides or talking behind people's backs.

This may sound daunting but in reality, it is very rare to find conflict between teaching staff and TAs that cannot be solved. There are further guidelines in Appendix 5.1 to help you think about your own practice and to ensure that channels of communication are used effectively.

Summary

Between 2003 and 2008 the Department for Children, Schools and Families commissioned a report into the impact of support staff on student outcomes. The DISS Project (Deployment and Impact of Support Staff) produced a report which made several recommendations, most of which echo points made above:

1. The need for careful consideration of conditions of employment so that support staff are appropriately rewarded.
2. The need to address aspects such as supervision and line management.

3. The need to prepare teachers, both newly qualified and in-service, with the skills to help manage support staff.

4. Make more time available for joint planning and feedback.

5. Deploy support staff to ensure that they don't routinely support lower attaining pupils and pupils with SEND.

6. Pupils in most need should get more, not less, of a teacher's time.

7. Teachers should take responsibility for the lesson-by-lesson curriculum and pedagogical planning for all pupils in the class, including those being supported by support staff.

8. More needs to be done on conceptualising the pedagogical role of support staff in their everyday interactions with pupils. It should be built in to professional development, school deployment decisions and the management, support and monitoring of support staff.

9. Schools need to set out explicitly and rigorously the quality of provision and support in relation to expected academic outcomes.

10. More research is needed which examines the effects not just of the amount of support (as in DISS) but of particular facets of the 'wider pedagogical role' of support staff on pupil learning, behaviour and attitudes to learning.

The full report can be accessed through http://maximisingtas.co.uk/research/the-diss-project.php

Notes

1 Case study from: www.teachernet.gov.uk/management/teachingassistants/Management/casestudies/

2 *Curriculum Close Up*, the RNIB Curriculum Information Service (01905 357635).

Appendix 1.1 SEND legislation

The Children and Families Act: A different landscape

The Children and Families Act 2014 introduced radical changes to the requirements placed on both schools and teachers regarding the education and inclusion of pupils with special educational needs and disabilities. The first major revision of the SEND framework for thirty years, it introduced a new system to help children with special educational needs and disabilities and shaped how education, health and social care professionals should work in partnership with children, young people and their families.

The reforms introduced a system to support children and young people from birth up to the age of 25, designed to ensure smooth transitions across all services as they move from school into further education, training and employment. The reforms give particular emphasis to preparing children and young people for adulthood from the earliest years. This means enabling children to be involved at as young an age as possible in all decisions relating to their learning, therapy, medical treatment and support from social care. The result of this preparation should be that when young people reach the age of 16, they are able to be full and active participants in all important decisions about their life.

> There is now an important distinction made between a child and a young person. The Act gives significant new rights directly to young people when they are over compulsory school age but under the age of 25. Under the Act, a child becomes a young person after the last day of summer term during the academic year in which he or she turns 16. This is subject to a young person 'having capacity' to take a decision under the Mental Capacity Act 2005.

Throughout this book the term 'pupils with special educational needs and disabilities (SEND)' is used. A pupil has special educational needs if he or she:

- has a significantly greater difficulty in learning than the majority of others of the same age; or
- has a disability which prevents or hinders him or her from making use of facilities of a kind generally provided for others of the same age in mainstream schools or mainstream post-16 institutions.

(SEND Code of Practice 2015: DfE 2015a)

Section 19 principles

Central to Part 3 of the Children and Families Act 2014 is Section 19. This section emphasises the role to be played by parents or carers and young people themselves, in all decision making about their SEND provision.

Part C of Section 19 issues a new challenge to schools in that there is a clear expectation that parents and pupils will not only be invited to participate but that they should be supported to do so. This will certainly involve the provision of relevant information to parents but schools could also consider providing other forms of support, both practical, such as helping with translation services, or transport to attend important meetings, and emotional, such as advocacy or pre-meetings to prepare parents and pupils to take a full part in all decisions. Many parents will need only a minimal level of additional support, but others, especially those often portrayed as 'hard to reach', may require considerably more.

Key questions:

- Do you know how your pupils with SEND and their parents feel about education, and what their wishes are? If not, how can you find out?
- What could you and others in your subject or departmental team do to integrate this information into your planning for and delivery of teaching and learning?
- What more could you do to reach out to parents who may be anxious about or unwilling to engage with school?

The SEND Code of Practice

As the quotation at the start of Chapter 1 makes clear, SEND provision is provision that is additional to or different from the high quality, differentiated teaching to which all pupils are entitled. A school's first response to a pupil falling behind his or her peers should be to evaluate the quality of teaching and learning the pupil currently receives in all subjects. The pupil should be identified as having SEND only when the school is confident that all teaching is differentiated appropriately to meet that individual pupil's needs.

Once a pupil is identified as having SEND, schools are required to do whatever they can to remove any barriers to learning and to put in place effective provision, or 'SEND support'. This support must enable pupils with SEND to achieve the best possible outcomes.

Most schools and academies welcome pupils with a range of vulnerabilities, including special educational needs and disabilities, but may hesitate about including those with significant or complex needs. The reasons behind this reluctance are often a lack of expertise in an area of need, worries about behaviour, and most commonly expressed, concerns about the impact of that pupil's needs on the education of others.

The SEND Code of Practice is very clear that where the parent of a pupil with an education, health and care plan (EHC plan) makes a request for a particular school, the local authority *must* comply with that preference and name the school in the plan unless:

- it would be unsuitable for the age, ability, aptitude or SEND of the child or young person, or
- the attendance of the child or young person there would be incompatible with the efficient education of others, or the efficient use of resources.

(DfE 2015a: 9.79 p. 172)

Legally, schools cannot refuse to admit a pupil who does not have an EHC plan on the grounds that either they do not feel able to cater for his or her needs, or the pupil does not have an EHC plan.

Outcomes

Outcomes are written from the perspective of the pupil and should identify what the provision is intended to achieve. For example, do you think the following is an outcome for a pupil in Year 7 with literacy difficulties?

> For the next ten weeks Jake will work on an online literacy program for 20 minutes three times each week.

It may be specific and measurable; it is achievable and realistic; and it is time targeted, so it is 'SMART' but it isn't an 'outcome'. What is described here is provision, i.e. the intervention that the school will use to help Jake to make accelerated progress.

Outcomes are intended to look forward to the end of the next stage or phase of education, usually two or three years hence. Teachers will, of course, set short term targets covering between six and 12 weeks and education and health plans will also include interim objectives to be discussed at annual reviews. So, what would be an outcome for Jake?

> By the end of Year 9, Jake will be able to read and understand the textbooks for his chosen GCSE courses.

The online literacy course would then form a part of the package of provision to enable Jake to achieve this outcome.

The graduated approach

The 2015 SEND Code of Practice describes SEND support as a cyclical process of assess, plan, do and review that is known as the 'graduated approach'. This cycle is already commonly used in schools, and for pupils with SEND it is intended to be much more than a token, in-house process. Rather it should be a powerful mechanism for reflection and evaluation of the impact of SEND provision. Through the four-part cycle, decisions and actions are revisited, refined and revised. This then leads to a deeper understanding of an individual pupil's needs whilst also offering an insight into the effectiveness of the school's overall provision for pupils with SEND. The graduated approach offers the school, the pupil and his or her parents a growing understanding of needs and of what provision the pupil requires to enable him or her to make good progress and secure good outcomes. Through successive cycles, the graduated approach draws on increasingly specialist expertise, assessments and approaches, and more frequent reviews. This structured process gives teachers the information they need to match specific, evidence-based interventions to pupils' individual needs.

Evidence-based interventions

In recent years, a number of universities and other research organisations have produced evidence about the efficacy of a range of different interventions for vulnerable pupils and pupils with SEND. Most notable among this research is that sponsored by the Education Endowment Fund that offers schools valid data on the impact of interventions and the optimal conditions for their use. Other important sources of information about evidence-based interventions for specific areas of need are the Communication Trust 'What Works?' website and 'Interventions for literacy' from the SpLD/Dyslexia Trust. Both sites offer transparent and clear information for professionals and parents to support joint decisions about provision.

The Equality Act 2010

Sitting alongside the Children and Families Act 2014, the requirements of the Equality Act 2010 remain firmly in place. This is especially important because many children and young people who have SEND may also have a disability under the Equality Act. The definition of disability in the Equality Act is that the child or young person has 'a physical or mental impairment which has a long-term and substantial adverse effect on a person's ability to carry out normal day-to-day activities'. 'Long-term' is defined as lasting or being likely to last for 'a year or more', and 'substantial' is defined as 'more than minor or trivial'. The definition includes sensory impairments such as those affecting sight or hearing, and, just as crucially for schools, children with long-term health conditions such as asthma, diabetes, epilepsy and cancer.

As the SEND Code of Practice (DfE 2015a: 16) states, the definition for disability provides a relatively low threshold, and includes many more children than schools may realise. Children and young people with some conditions do not necessarily have SEND, but there is often a significant overlap between disabled children and young people, and those with SEND. Where a disabled child or young person requires special educational provision they will also be covered by the SEND duties.

The Equality Act applies to all schools including academies and free schools, university technical colleges and studio schools, and also further education colleges and sixth form colleges – even where the school or college has no disabled pupils currently on roll. This is because the duties under the Equality Act are anticipatory in that they cover not only current pupils but also prospective ones. The expectation is that all schools will be reviewing accessibility continually and making reasonable adjustments in order to improve access for disabled pupils. When thinking about disabled access, the first thing that school leaders usually consider is physical access, such as wheelchair access, lifts and ramps. But physical access is only part of the requirement of the Equality Act and often is the simplest to improve. Your school's accessibility plan for disabled pupils must address all of three elements of planned improvements in access:

1. physical improvements to increase access to education and associated services;
2. improvements in access to the curriculum;
3. improvements in the provision of information for disabled pupils in a range of formats.

Improvements in access to the curriculum are often a harder nut to crack as they involve all departments and all teachers looking closely at their teaching and learning strategies and evaluating how effectively these meet the needs of disabled pupils. Often, relatively minor amendments to the curriculum or teaching approaches can lead to major improvements in access for disabled pupils and these often have a positive impact on the education of all pupils. For example, one school installed a Soundfield amplification system in a number of classrooms because a pupil with a hearing loss had joined the school. The following year, the cohort of Year 7 pupils had particularly poor speaking and listening skills and it was noticed that they were more engaged in learning when they were taught in the rooms with the Soundfield system. This led to improvements in progress for the whole cohort and significantly reduced the level of disruption and off-task behaviours in those classes.

Schools also have wider duties under the Equality Act to prevent discrimination, to promote equality of opportunity and to foster good relations. These duties should inform all aspects of school improvement planning from curriculum design through to anti-bullying policies and practice.

Significantly, a pupil's underachievement or behaviour difficulties might relate to an underlying physical or mental impairment which could be covered by the Equality Act. Each pupil is different and will respond to situations in his or her unique way so a disability should be considered in the context of the child as an individual. The 'social model' of disability sees the environment as the primary disabling factor, as opposed to the 'medical model' that focuses on the individual child's needs and difficulties. School activities and environments should be considered in the light of possible barriers to learning or participation.

Appendix 1.2 Departmental policy

Whether the practice in your school is to have separate SEND policies for each department or to embed the information on SEND in your whole-school inclusion or teaching and learning policies, the processes and information detailed below will still be relevant.

Good practice for pupils with SEND and disabilities is good practice for all pupils, especially those who are 'vulnerable' to underachievement. Vulnerable groups may include looked-after children (CLA), pupils for whom English is an additional language (EAL), pupils from minority ethnic groups, young carers and pupils known to be eligible for free school meals/ Pupil Premium funding. Be especially aware of those pupils with SEND who face one or more additional vulnerabilities and for whom effective support might need to go beyond help in the classroom.

It is crucial that your departmental or faculty policy describes a strategy for meeting pupils' special educational needs within your particular curricular area. The policy should set the scene for any visitor, from supply staff to inspectors, and make a valuable contribution to the departmental handbook. The process of developing a department SEND policy offers the opportunity to clarify and evaluate current thinking and practice within the MFL team and to establish a consistent approach.

The SEND policy for your department is a significant document in terms of the leadership and management of your subject. The preparation and review of the policy should be led by a senior manager within the team because that person needs to have sufficient status to be able to influence subsequent practice and training across the department.

What should a departmental policy contain?

The starting points for your departmental SEND policy will be the whole-school SEND policy and the SEND Information Report that, under the Children and

Families Act 2014, all schools are required to publish. Each subject department's own policy should then 'flesh out' the detail in a way that describes how things will work in practice. Writing the policy needs to be much more than a paper exercise completed merely to satisfy the senior management team and Ofsted inspectors. Rather, it is an opportunity for your staff to come together as a team to create a framework for teaching MFL in a way that makes your subject accessible, not only to pupils with special educational needs and disabilities, but for all pupils in the school. It is also an ideal opportunity to discuss the impact of grouping on academic and social outcomes for pupils. Bear in mind that the Code of Practice includes a specific duty that 'schools must ensure that children and young people with SEN engage in the activities of the school alongside pupils who do not have SEN' (DfE 2015a: 6.2 p. 92).

We need to be careful in MFL that when grouping pupils, we are not bound solely by measures in reading and writing, but also take into account comprehension and oral language abilities. It is vital that social issues are also taken into account if pupils are to be able to learn effectively. Having a complement of pupils with good oral ability will lift the attitude and attainment of everybody within a group.

Who should be involved in developing our SEND policy?

The job of developing and reviewing your policy will be easier if tackled as a joint endeavour. Involve people who will be able to offer support and guidance such as:

- the school SEND governor;
- the SENCO or other school leader with responsibility for SEND;
- your support staff, including teaching assistants and technicians;
- the school data manager, who will be able to offer information about the attainment and progress of different groups;
- outside experts from your local authority, academy chain or other schools
- parents of pupils with SEND;
- pupils themselves – both with and without SEND.

Bringing together a range of views and information will enable you to develop a policy that is compliant with the letter *and* principle of the legislation, that is relevant to the context of your school and that is useful in guiding practice and improving outcomes for all pupils.

The role of parents in developing your department SEND policy

As outlined in Appendix 1.1, Section 19 of the Children and Families Act 2014 raises the bar of expectations about how parents should be involved in and influence the work of schools. Not only is it best practice to involve parents of pupils with SEND in the development of policy, but it will also help in 'getting it right' for both pupils and staff. There are a number of ways, both formal and informal, to find out the views of parents to inform policy writing, including:

- a focus group;
- a coffee morning/drop-in;
- a questionnaire/online survey;
- a phone survey of a sample of parents.

Parents will often respond more readily if the request for feedback or invitation to attend a meeting comes from their son or daughter.

Where to start when writing a policy

An audit can act as a starting point for reviewing current policy on SEND or writing a new policy. This will involve gathering information and reviewing current practice with regard to pupils with SEND, and is best completed by the whole department, preferably with some input from the SENCO or another member of staff with responsibility for SEND within the school. An audit carried out by the whole department provides a valuable opportunity for professional development so long as it is seen as an exercise in sharing good practice and encourages joint planning. It may also facilitate your department's contribution to the school provision map. But before embarking on an audit, it is worth investing some time in a departmental meeting, or ideally a training day, to raise awareness of the legislation around special educational needs and disabilities and to establish a shared philosophy across your department.

The following headings may be useful when you are establishing your departmental policy:

General statement of compliance

- What is the overarching aim of the policy? What outcomes do you want to achieve for pupils with SEND?
- How are you complying with legislation and guidance?
- What does the school SEND Information Report say about teaching and learning and provision for pupils with SEND?

> ### Example
>
> All members of the department will ensure that the needs of all pupils with SEND are met, according to the aims of the school and its SEND policy . . .

Definition of SEND

- What does SEND mean?
- What are the areas of need and the categories used in the Code of Practice?
- Are there any special implications for our subject area?

(See Chapter 1.)

Provision for staff within the department

- Who has responsibility for SEND within the department?
- What are the responsibilities of this role?

  e.g.

  - liaison between the department and the SENCO;
  - monitoring the progress of and outcomes for pupils with SEND, e.g. identifying attainment gaps between pupils with SEND and their peers;
  - attending any liaison meetings and providing feedback to colleagues;
  - attending and contributing to training;
  - maintaining departmental SEND information and records;
  - representing the needs of pupils with SEND at departmental level;
  - liaising with parents of pupils with SEND;
  - gathering feedback from pupils with SEND on the impact of teaching and support strategies on their learning and well-being.

(This post can be seen as a valuable development opportunity for staff and the name of this person should be included in the policy. However, where responsibility for SEND is given to a relatively junior member of the team, there must be support and supervision from the head of the department to ensure that the needs of pupils with SEND have sufficient prominence in both policy and practice.)

- What information about pupils' SEND is held, where is it stored and how is it shared?
- How can staff access additional resources, information and training?
- How will staff ensure effective planning and communication between teachers and teaching assistants?
- What assessments are available for teachers in your department to support accurate identification of SEND?

Example

The member of staff with responsibility for overseeing the provision of SEND within the department will attend liaison meetings and subsequently give feedback to the other members of the department. S/he will maintain the department's SEND file, attend and/or organise appropriate training and disseminate this to all departmental staff. All information will be treated with confidentiality.

Provision for pupils with SEND

- How are pupils' special educational needs identified?

  e.g.

  - observation in lessons;
  - assessment of class work/homework;
  - end of module tests/progress checks;
  - annual examinations/SATs/GCSE;
  - reports.

- How is progress measured for pupils with SEND?
- How do members of the department contribute to individual learning plans, meetings with parents and reviews?
- What criteria are used for organising teaching groups?
- How/when can pupils move between groups?
- What adjustments are made for pupils with special educational needs and/ or disabilities in lessons and homework?
- How do we use information about pupils' abilities in reading, writing, speaking and listening when planning lessons and homework?
- What alternative courses are available for pupils with SEND?
- What special arrangements are made for internal and external examinations?
- What guidance is available for working effectively with support staff?

Here is a good place also to put a statement about the school behaviour policy and any rewards and sanctions, and how the department will make any necessary adjustments to meet the needs of pupils with SEND.

> **Example**
>
> The staff in the MFL department will aim to support pupils with SEND to achieve the best possible outcomes. They will do this by supporting pupils to achieve their individual targets as specified in their individual learning plans, and will provide feedback for progress reviews. Pupils with SEND will be included in the departmental monitoring system used for all pupils.

Resources and learning materials

- Is any specialist equipment used in the department?
- How are differentiated resources developed? What criteria do we use (e.g. literacy levels)?
- Where are resources stored and are they accessible for both staff and pupils?

> **Example**
>
> The department will provide suitably differentiated materials and where appropriate, specialist resources to meet the needs of pupils with SEND. Alternative courses and examinations will be made available where appropriate for individual pupils. Support staff will be provided with curriculum information in advance of lessons and will be involved in lesson planning. A list of resources is available in the department handbook.

Staff qualifications and continuing professional development (CPD)

- What qualifications and experience do the members of the department have?
- What training has already taken place, and when? What impact did that training have on teaching and learning, and progress for pupils with SEND?
- How is training planned? What criteria are used to identify training needs?
- How are SEND taken into account when new training opportunities are proposed?
- Is a record kept of training completed and on-going training needs?

> **Example**
>
> A record of training undertaken, specialist skills and training required will be kept in the department handbook. Requests for training will be considered in line with the department and school improvement plan.

Monitoring and reviewing the policy

- How will the policy be monitored?
- Who will lead the monitoring?
- When will the policy be reviewed?

> **Example**
>
> The department SEND policy will be monitored by the head of department on a planned annual basis, with advice being sought from the SENCO as part of the three-yearly review process.

Conclusion

Creating a departmental SEND policy should be a developmental activity that will improve teaching and learning for all pupils, but especially for those who are vulnerable to underachievement. The policy should be a working document that will evolve and change over time; it is there to challenge current practice and to encourage improvement for both pupils and staff. If departmental staff work together to create the policy, they will have ownership of it; it will have true meaning and be effective in clarifying good practice.

An example of a departmental policy for you to amend is available in the eResources for this book at www.routledge.com/9781138699281

Appendix 1.3 Different types of SEND

Introduction

This appendix is a starting point for information on the special educational needs most frequently encountered in mainstream schools. It describes the main characteristics of each area of special educational need and disability (SEND), with practical ideas for use in the teaching of modern languages, and contacts for further information.

There is a measure of repetition, as some strategies prove to be effective with a whole range of pupils (and often with those who have no identified SEND). However, the layout provides readers with an 'at a glance' reminder of effective approaches and facilitates copying for colleagues and TAs.

The SEND Code of Practice (DfE 2015a) outlines four broad areas of need. These are:

- communication and interaction;
- cognition and learning;
- social, emotional and mental health difficulties;
- sensory and/or physical needs.

These broad areas are not exclusive and pupils may have needs that cut across some or all of them. Equally, pupils' difficulties and needs will change over time. The terms used in this chapter are helpful when reviewing and monitoring special educational provision but pupils' individual talents and interests are just as important as their disability or special educational need. Because of this, specific terms or labels need to be used with care in discussion with parents, pupils or other professionals. Unless a pupil has a firm diagnosis, and parents and pupil understand the implications of that diagnosis, it is more appropriate to describe the features of the special educational need rather than use the label. For example a teacher might describe a pupil's spelling difficulties but not use the term 'dyslexic'.

There is a continuum of need within each of the special educational needs and disabilities listed here. Some pupils will be affected more than others, and show fewer or more of the characteristics described.

Pupils with other, less common special educational needs may be included in some schools, and additional information on these conditions may be found in a variety of sources. These include the school SENCO, local authority support services, educational psychologists and online information, for example on the Nasen SEND Gateway and disability charity websites such as Mencap, CAF or I CAN, the children's communication charity.

Further information

www.nasen.org.uk
www.mencap.org.uk
www.cafamily.org.uk
www.ican.org.uk

Attention deficit disorder (with or without hyperactivity) ADD/ADHD

Attention deficit hyperactivity disorder is one of the most common childhood disorders and can continue through adolescence and adulthood. ADHD can occur in pupils of any intellectual ability and may also cause additional problems, such as sleep and anxiety disorders. The features of ADHD usually diminish with age, but many individuals who are diagnosed with the condition at a young age will continue to experience problems in adulthood.

Main characteristics

- short attention span or easily distracted by noise and movement
- difficulty in following instructions and completing tasks
- difficulty in listening to and processing verbal instructions
- restlessness, inability to keep still, causing frequent fidgeting
- difficulty with moderating behaviour such as constant talking, interrupting and calling out
- difficulty in waiting or taking turns
- impulsivity – acting without thinking about consequences

How can the modern languages teacher help?

- Make eye contact and use the pupil's name when speaking to him.
- Keep instructions simple – the one sentence rule.
- Provide clear written instruction.
- Position the pupil away from obvious distractions e.g. windows, computer screens.
- Provide clear routines and rules, and rehearse them regularly.
- Encourage the pupil to repeat instructions (to you or TA) before starting work.
- Tell the pupil when to begin a task.
- Give two choices – avoid the option of the pupil saying 'no': e.g. 'Do you want to write in blue or black pen?'
- Give advanced warning when something is about to happen. Signal a change or finish with a time, e.g. 'In two minutes I need you (pupil name) to . . .'.
- Give specific praise – catch him being good, give attention for positive behaviour.
- Give the pupil responsibilities so that others can see him in a positive light and he develops a positive self-image.

Further information

ADDISS	020 8952 2800	www.addiss.co.uk
ADHD Foundation	0151 237 2661	www.adhdfoundation.org.uk
Young Minds	020 7089 5050	www.youngminds.org.uk

Autism (ASD)

Asperger's Syndrome

Asperger's Syndrome is a type of autism. People with Asperger's Syndrome do not have 'learning difficulties' as such, but they do have difficulties associated with being on the autistic spectrum. They often want to make friends but do not understand the complex rules of social interaction. They may have impaired fine and gross motor skills, with writing being a particular problem. Boys are more likely to be affected, with the ratio being 10:1 boys to girls. Because they appear 'odd' and naïve, these pupils are particularly vulnerable to bullying.

Main characteristics

- **Social interaction**
  Pupils with Asperger's Syndrome want friends but have not developed the strategies necessary for making and sustaining meaningful friendships. They find it very difficult to learn social norms and to pick up on social cues. Social situations, such as assemblies and less formal lessons, can cause great anxiety.

- **Social communication**
  Pupils have appropriate spoken language but tend to sound formal and pedantic, using limited expression and possibly with an unusual tone of voice. They have difficulty in using and understanding non-verbal language such as facial expression, gesture, body language and eye contact. They may have a literal understanding of language and do not grasp implied meanings.

- **Social imagination**
  Pupils with Asperger's Syndrome need structured environments, and to have routines they understand and can anticipate. They may excel at learning facts but have difficulty in understanding abstract concepts and in generalising information and skills. They often have all-consuming special interests.

How can the modern languages teacher help?

- Liaise closely with parents, especially over homework.
- Create as calm a classroom environment as possible.
- Allow to sit in the same place for each lesson.
- Set up a work buddy system for your lessons.
- Provide additional visual cues in class, such as visual timetables and task activity lists.
- Give the pupil time to process questions and respond.
- Make sure pupils understand what you expect of them.

- Offer alternatives to handwriting for recording work.
- Prepare pupils for changes to routines well in advance.
- Give written homework instructions.
- Have your own class rules and apply them consistently.

Further information

www.autism.org.uk/about/what-is/asperger.aspx

Autistic spectrum disorder (ASD)

Autism is a developmental disability that affects how a person communicates with, and relates to, other people. It also affects how they make sense of the world around them. It is often referred to as a spectrum or ASD, which means that, while all people with autism share certain difficulties, the condition may affect them in different ways. Pupils with ASD cover the full range of academic ability and the severity of the disability varies widely. Some pupils also have learning disabilities or other difficulties, such as dyslexia. Four times as many boys as girls are diagnosed with an ASD.

Main characteristics

- **Social interaction**
  Pupils with ASD find it difficult to understand social behaviour and this affects their ability to interact with others. They do not always understand social contexts. They may experience high levels of stress and anxiety in settings that do not meet their needs or when routines are changed. This can lead to inappropriate behaviour.

- **Social communication**
  Understanding and use of non-verbal and verbal communication is impaired. Pupils with an ASD have difficulties understanding the communication of others and in developing effective communication themselves. They may have a literal understanding of language. Many are delayed in learning to speak, and some people with ASD never develop speech at all.

- **Social imagination and flexibility of thought**
  Pupils with an ASD have difficulty in thinking and behaving flexibly, which may result in restricted, obsessional or repetitive activities. They are often more interested in objects than in people, and have intense interests in such things as trains and vacuum cleaners. Pupils work best when they have a routine. Unexpected changes in those routines will cause distress. Some pupils with autistic spectrum disorders have a different perception of sounds, sights, smell, touch and taste, and this can affect their response to these sensations.

How can the modern languages teacher help?

- Collaborate closely with parents as they will have many useful strategies.
- Provide visual supports in class: objects, pictures, a symbol timetable, etc.
- Always consider potential sensory issues.
- Give advance warning of any changes to usual routines.
- Provide either an individual desk or the opportunity to work with a buddy.

- Take into account the pupil's individual learning style and preferences, e.g. by allowing for a choice of output for a task: a digital recording, a short video, a drawing, a photograph with caption, a word-processed document, an e-book, a mini-book.
- Give individual instructions using the pupil's name at the beginning of the request, e.g. 'Paul, bring me your book'.
- Be alert to pupils' levels of anxiety.
- Develop social interactions using a buddy system or circle of friends.
- Avoid using metaphor, idiom or sarcasm – say what you mean in simple language.
- Use pupils' special interests as motivations.
- Help pupils to manage potentially difficult situations by rehearsing them beforehand (perhaps with a TA) or through the use of social stories.

Further information

| The National Autistic Society | 020 7833 2299 | www.autism.org.uk |
| Autism Education Trust | 0207 903 3650 | www.autismeducationtrust.org.uk |

Cerebral palsy (CP)

Cerebral palsy is a condition that affects muscle control and movement. It is usually caused by an injury to the brain before, during or after birth. Pupils with cerebral palsy have difficulties in controlling their muscles and movements as they grow and develop. Problems vary from slight clumsiness to more severe lack of control of movements. Pupils with CP may also have learning difficulties. They may use a wheelchair or other mobility aid.

Main characteristics

There are three main forms of cerebral palsy:

- **spastic cerebral palsy** – associated with stiff or tight muscle tone resulting in a decreased range of movement. This stiffening of muscle tone can be very painful and affect different parts of the body;
- **dyskinetic cerebral palsy** – sustained or intermittent involuntary muscle contractions often affecting the whole body;
- **ataxic cerebral palsy** – an inability to activate the correct pattern of muscles during movement resulting in an unsteady gait with balance difficulties and poor spatial awareness.

Pupils with CP may also have communication difficulties.

How can the modern languages teacher help?

- Gather information from parents and therapists involved with the pupil (perhaps via the SENCO until parents' evening provides an opportunity for a face-to-face chat).
- Consider the classroom layout to maximise access.
- Have high academic expectations.
- Use visual supports: objects, pictures, symbols.
- Arrange a work or subject buddy.
- Speak directly to the pupil rather than through a teaching assistant.
- Ensure access to appropriate IT equipment for language learning and check that it is used effectively.
- Consider late arrival to and early exit from lessons to avoid potential problems in crowded corridors.

Further information

Scope   0808 800 3333   www.scope.org.uk

Down's syndrome

Down's syndrome (DS) is the most common identifiable cause of learning disability. This is a genetic condition caused by the presence of an extra chromosome 21. People with DS have varying degrees of learning difficulties ranging from mild to severe. They have a specific learning profile with characteristic strengths and weaknesses. All share certain physical characteristics but will also inherit family traits, in physical features and personality. They may have additional sight, hearing, respiratory and heart problems.

Main characteristics

- delayed motor skills
- taking longer to learn and consolidate new skills
- limited concentration
- difficulties with generalisation, thinking and reasoning
- sequencing difficulties
- stronger visual than aural skills
- better social than academic skills

How can the modern languages teacher help?

- Ensure that the pupil can see and hear you and other pupils.
- Speak directly to the pupil and reinforce speech with facial expression, pictures and objects.
- Use simple, familiar language in short sentences.
- Check instructions have been understood.
- Give the pupil time to process information and formulate a response.
- Break lessons up into a series of shorter, varied and achievable tasks.
- Accept alternative ways of responding to tasks: drawings, audio or video recordings, symbols, etc.
- Set individual tasks linked to the work of the rest of the class.
- Provide age-appropriate resources and activities.
- Allow the pupil to work with more able peers to give good models of work and behaviour.
- Provide a work buddy.
- Expect the pupil to work unsupported for part of every lesson to avoid over-dependence on adult support.

Further information

| Down's Syndrome Association | 020 8682400 | www.downs-syndrome.org.uk |

Foetal alcohol syndrome

Foetal alcohol syndrome (FAS) or foetal alcohol spectrum disorders (FASD) are umbrella terms for diagnoses relating to a child's exposure to alcohol before birth. Alcohol can affect the development of all cells and organs but it is the brain and nervous system that are particularly vulnerable. Each person with FAS/D may face a range of difficulties across a spectrum from mild to severe.

Main characteristics

- visual impairment
- sleep problems
- speech and language delay
- impulsivity and or hyperactivity
- memory problems
- inappropriate social behaviour

How can the modern languages teacher help?

- Gather information from parents and other professionals involved with the pupil to find the most effective ways of teaching him/her (perhaps through the SENCO in the first instance).
- Find out the pupil's strengths and use these as starting points for learning.
- Keep instructions simple and offer information in verbal and visual form, supported by mime, gesture and facial expression.
- Ask another pupil to confirm in English any instructions given in the target language.
- Ensure class routines are explicit and followed consistently.
- Use concrete and positive language, e.g. 'Walk' rather than 'Don't run'.
- Check the pupil knows and understands any school or class rules.
- Specify clearly what is expected for any task or activity.
- Provide a memory mat or audio recording facilities to support retention of information, e.g. homework tasks, spelling, etc.

Further information

www.drinkaware.co.uk/fas

Learning disability (learning difficulty)

The terms 'learning disability' and 'learning difficulty' are used to describe a wide continuum of difficulties ranging from moderate (MLD) to profound and multiple (PMLD). Pupils with learning disabilities find it harder to understand, learn and remember new things, meaning they may have problems across a range of areas such as communication, being aware of risks or managing everyday tasks.

Moderate learning difficulties (MLD)

The term 'moderate learning difficulties' is used to describe pupils who find it extremely difficult to achieve expected levels of attainment across the curriculum, even with a well-differentiated and flexible approach to teaching. These pupils do not find learning easy and can suffer from low self-esteem and sometimes exhibit unacceptable behaviour as a way of avoiding failure. For all pupils with learning disabilities, the social aspect of school is a crucial element in their development and understanding of the 'culture' of young people, so it is important for them to have friends who don't have learning disabilities as well as those who do. As the SEND Code of Practice says at 6.2 (p. 92): 'Schools must . . . ensure that children and young people with SEN engage in the activities of the school alongside pupils who do not have SEN.'

Main characteristics

- difficulties with reading, writing and comprehension
- problems understanding and retaining mathematical skills and concepts
- immature social and emotional skills
- limited vocabulary and communication skills
- short attention span
- underdeveloped co-ordination skills
- inability to transfer and apply skills to different situations
- difficulty remembering what has been taught previously
- difficulty with personal organisation such as following a timetable, remembering books and equipment

How can the modern languages teacher help?

- Find out about the pupil's strengths, interests and areas of weakness.
- Have high expectations.
- Establish a routine within your lessons.
- Base your planning around a reduced core of topic-specific language and recycle that language in as many different formats as possible: flashcard games, appropriate technology, use of TPR (total physical response) approaches, songs, rhymes.

- Keep tasks short and varied.
- Keep listening tasks short or broken up with other activities.
- Provide word lists, writing frames and shortened versions of text to be read.
- Offer alternative methods of recording information, e.g. drawings, charts, labelling, diagrams, use of technology.
- Check previously gained knowledge and build on this (it may be at a very different level from that of other pupils in the class).
- Offer instructions and information in different ways, e.g. use a cartoon avatar with voice-over to introduce the lesson (see www.voki.com); use an electronic poster to present information (see www.glogster.com).
- Be explicit about the expected outcome; demonstrate or show examples of completed work. WAGOLL it (What A Good One Looks Like).
- Use practical, concrete, visual examples to illustrate explanations.
- Question the pupil to check he has grasped a concept or has understood instructions.
- Make sure the pupil always has something to do.
- Use lots of praise, instant rewards, catch them trying hard.
- Make sure you praise the effort involved rather than overpraising outcomes that are pretty ordinary. Use language such as 'Good start. Is there anything we can do to improve it?' Carol Dweck refers to the 'power of "yet" over the tyranny of "now"'. Ensure that pupils get the message that even if the outcome isn't particularly special, there is always something we can do to improve – we're not there 'yet'.

Severe learning difficulties (SLD)

This term covers a wide and varied group of pupils who have significant intellectual or cognitive impairments. Many have communication difficulties and/or sensory impairments in addition to more general learning difficulties. Some pupils may also have difficulties in mobility, coordination and perception and the use of signs and symbols will be helpful to support their communication and understanding. Pupils' academic attainment will also vary with many able to access a well-differentiated mainstream curriculum and achieve at GCSE level.

How can the modern languages teacher help?

- Liaise with parents (perhaps through the SENCO in the first instance).
- Arrange a work/subject buddy.
- Use visual supports: objects, pictures, symbols.
- Learn some signs relevant to the teaching of languages, e.g. Makaton.
- Allow time for pupils to process information and formulate responses.
- Set differentiated tasks linked to the work of the rest of the class.

- Set achievable targets for each lesson or module of work.
- Accept different recording methods: drawings, audio or video recordings, photographs, etc.
- Give access to computers where appropriate.
- Plan a series of short, varied activities within each lesson.

Profound and multiple learning difficulties (PMLD)

Pupils with profound and multiple learning difficulties have complex learning needs. In addition to severe learning difficulties, pupils have other significant difficulties, such as physical disabilities, sensory impairments or severe medical conditions. Pupils with PMLD require a high level of adult support, both for their learning needs and for personal care.

Pupils with PMLD are able to access the curriculum largely through sensory experiences. Some pupils communicate by gesture, eye pointing or symbols, others by very simple language. The concept of progress for pupils with PMLD covers more than academic attainment. Indeed, for some pupils who may have associated medical conditions, simply maintaining knowledge and skills will count as good progress.

How can the modern languages teacher help?

- Work closely with teaching/support assistants working with the pupil.
- Consider the classroom layout so that wheelchairs can move around easily and safely.
- Identify all possible sensory opportunities in your lessons.
- Use additional sensory supports: objects, pictures, fragrances, music, textures, food, etc., e.g. the French word *une orange* is better understood if the pupil can feel an orange in the hand and taste a segment or two, with an orange essential oil in a burner in the background (risk assessed, of course!).
- Use photographs to record the pupil's experiences and responses.
- Set up a work/subject buddy rota for the class.
- Identify opportunities for the pupil to work in groups.

Further information

Mencap	020 7454 0454	www.mencap.org.uk
Foundation for People with Learning Disabilities	020 7803 1100	www.learningdisabilities.org.uk

Physical disability (PD)

There is a wide range of physical disabilities, and pupils with PD span all academic abilities. Some pupils are able to access the curriculum and learn effectively without additional educational provision. They have a disability but do not have a special educational need. For other pupils, the impact of their disability on their education may be significant, and the school will need to make adjustments to enable access to the curriculum.

Some pupils with a physical disability have associated medical conditions that may have an impact on their mobility. These conditions include cerebral palsy, heart disease, spina bifida and muscular dystrophy. They may also have sensory impairments, neurological problems or learning disabilities. They may use a wheelchair and/or additional mobility aids. Some pupils will be mobile but may have significant fine motor difficulties that require support or specialist resources. Others may need augmentative or alternative communication aids.

Pupils with a physical disability may need to miss lessons to attend physiotherapy or medical appointments. They are also likely to become very tired as they expend greater effort to complete everyday tasks. Teachers need to be flexible and sensitive to individual pupil needs.

How can the modern languages teacher help?

- Get to know the pupil (and parents) so that they will help you make the right adjustments.
- Maintain high expectations.
- Consider the classroom layout.
- Give permission for the pupil to leave lessons a few minutes early to avoid busy corridors and give time to get to the next lesson.
- Set homework earlier in the lesson so instructions are not missed.
- Speak directly to the pupil rather than through a teaching assistant.
- Let pupils make their own decisions.
- Ensure access to appropriate IT equipment for the lesson and check that it is used.
- Offer alternative ways of recording work.
- Plan to cover work missed through illness or medical appointments.
- Be sensitive to fatigue, especially towards the end of the school day.

Further information

Scope   0808 800 3333   www.scope.org.uk

Social, emotional and mental health difficulties

This area includes pupils who experience a wide range of difficulties characterised in a number of ways, including becoming withdrawn or by exhibiting behavioural difficulties. Behaviours such as these may reflect underlying mental health difficulties including depression, anxiety and eating disorders. These difficulties can be seen across the whole ability range and have a continuum of severity. Attachment disorders and attention deficit disorder will also be part of this continuum. Pupils with special educational needs in this area are those who have persistent difficulties despite the school having in place an effective school behaviour policy and a robust personal and social curriculum.

Main characteristics

- inattentive, poor concentration and lacking interest in school and school work
- easily frustrated and anxious about changes
- difficulty working in groups
- unable to work independently, constantly seeking help or attention
- confrontational: verbally aggressive towards pupils and/or adults
- physically aggressive towards pupils and/or adults
- destroys property: their own and that of others
- appears withdrawn, distressed, unhappy, or sulky, and may self-harm
- lacks confidence and self-esteem
- may find it difficult to communicate
- finds it difficult to accept praise

How can the modern languages teacher help?

- Check the ability level of the pupil and adapt expectations of work accordingly.
- Consider the pupil's strengths and interests and use these as motivators.
- Tell the pupil clearly what you expect in advance, for work and for behaviour.
- Talk to the pupil to find out more about them and how they feel about learning.
- Set a subject target with a reward system, e.g. the target language raffle: for each utterance the pupil volunteers in the target language, give one raffle ticket. At the end of a pre-determined period (half-term, term) hold the raffle, making sure that the prize is something tangible and worth winning, such as a cinema ticket, Easter egg, mp3 player. It's amazing what some firms will donate as raffle prizes. Consider using Classdojo as a real-time behaviour management system. This will allow you to feed back to the pupil at the end of each lesson as to how well (or otherwise) they have met the agreed criteria. It could be participation, asking questions, not talking out of turn, etc.

- Focus your comments on the behaviour not on the pupil ('That was a rude thing to say' rather than 'You are a rude boy').
- Use positive language and gestures and verbal praise whenever possible.
- Tell the pupil what you want them to do: 'I need you to . . .', 'I want you to . . .' rather than ask, 'Will you . . .?' This avoids confrontation and the possibility that there is room for negotiation.
- Give the pupil a choice between two options.
- Stick to what you say. Be consistent.
- Give the pupil class responsibilities to increase self-esteem and confidence.
- Plan a 'time out' system; ask a colleague for help with this.

Further information

SEBDA   01233 622958   www.sebda.org

Sensory impairments

Hearing impairment (HI)

The term 'hearing impairment' is a generic term used to describe all hearing loss. The main types of loss are monaural, conductive, sensory and mixed loss. The degree of hearing loss is described as mild, moderate, severe or profound.

How can the modern languages teacher help?

- Find out about the degree of the pupil's hearing loss and the likely implications for your lessons.
- Allocate the most appropriate seating position for the pupil (e.g. away from the hum of computers, with the better ear towards the speaker).
- Check that the pupil can see your face for facial expressions and lip reading.
- Make sure the light falls on your face and lips. Do not stand with your back to a window.
- Provide a list of vocabulary, context and visual clues, especially for new subjects.
- During class discussion allow one pupil to speak at a time and indicate where the speaker is.
- Check that any aids are working.
- If you use interactive whiteboards, ensure that the beam does not prevent the pupil from seeing your face.

Further information

| Action on Hearing Loss | 020 7296 8000 | www.actiononhearingloss.org.uk |
| The National Deaf Children's Society | 020 7490 8656 | www.ndcs.org.uk |

Visual impairment (VI)

Visual impairment refers to a range of difficulties and includes the disabilities of those pupils with monocular vision (vision in one eye), those who are partially sighted and those who are blind. Pupils with visual impairment cover the whole ability range and some pupils may have additional special educational needs.

How can the modern languages teacher help?

- Check the optimum position for the pupil, e.g. for a monocular pupil their good eye should be towards the action.
- If you move around the classroom give the pupil an aural cue as to where you are, e.g. by snapping your fingers, or using a clicker before you speak.
- Always provide the pupil with his own copy of any texts, with enlarged print where possible.
- Check accessibility of IT systems (enlarged icons, screen readers, etc.).
- Do not stand with your back to the window as this creates a silhouette and makes it harder for the pupil to see you.
- Draw the pupil's attention to displays, which they may not notice.
- Make sure the floor is kept free of clutter.
- Let the pupil know if there is a change to the layout of a space.
- Ask if there is any specialist equipment that the pupil requires for your subject, such as enlarged print dictionaries or additional lighting.

Further information

Royal National Institute for Blind People RNIB   0303 123 9999   www.rnib.org.uk

---

Multi-sensory impairment (MSI)

Pupils with multi-sensory impairment have a combination of visual and hearing difficulties. They may also have other additional disabilities that make their situation complex. A pupil with these difficulties is likely to need a high level of individual support.

How can the modern languages teacher help?

- Liaise with specialist teachers and support staff to ascertain the appropriate provision within your subject.
- Learn how to use alternative means of communication, as appropriate.
- Be prepared to be flexible and to adapt tasks, targets and assessment procedures.

Specific learning difficulties (SpLD)

The term 'specific learning difficulties' includes dyslexia, dyscalculia and dyspraxia.

Dyslexia

The term 'dyslexia' is used to describe difficulties that affect the ability to learn to read, write and/or spell stemming from a difficulty in processing the sounds in words. Although found across a whole range of ability, pupils with dyslexia often have strengths in reasoning and in visual and creative skills, but their particular difficulties can result in underachievement in school. While pupils can learn strategies to manage the effects of dyslexia, it is a life-long condition and its effects may be amplified at times of stress or in unfamiliar situations.

Main characteristics

- The pupil may frequently lose his place while reading, make errors with even high frequency words and have difficulty reading names, blending sounds and segmenting words. Reading and writing require a great deal of effort and concentration.
- Written work may seem messy with uneven letters and crossings out. Similarly shaped letters may be confused, such as b/d/p/q, m/w, n/u and letters in words may be jumbled, such as tired/tried. Spelling difficulties often persist into adult life and these pupils can become reluctant writers.
- Personal organisation can be underdeveloped.

How can the modern languages teacher help?

- Be aware of the pupil's individual strengths and areas of difficulty – speak to him directly to identify effective support strategies.
- Teach and encourage the use of IT, such as spell-checkers, predictive text, screen-readers, etc.
- Make sure pupils have the 'big picture' for the lesson/topic.
- Make sure that there is a strong emphasis on phoneme/grapheme relationships in lessons.
- Provide word lists and photocopies rather than expect the pupil to copy from the board.
- Colour-code word lists by gender to aid memory.
- Link words and phrases to physical movements.
- Use a sequence of multilink or Lego bricks as a prompt for sentence structure.
- Place cut-out foot shapes on the floor for pupils to 'walk through' a sentence.

- Consider alternatives to lengthy pieces of writing, e.g. pictures, plans, flow charts, mind maps, podcasts, etc.
- Allow extra time for tasks including assessments and examinations.
- Support the pupil in recording homework to be completed – and time scales.

Further information

www.dyslexiaaction.org.uk

Dyscalculia

The term 'dyscalculia' is used to describe difficulties in processing number concepts and mastering basic numeracy skills. These difficulties might be in marked contrast to the pupil's developmental level and general ability in other areas.

Main characteristics

- The pupil may have difficulty in counting by rote, writing or reading numbers, may miss out or reverse numbers, have difficulty with mental maths, and be unable to remember concepts, rules and formulae.
- In maths-based concepts, the pupil may have difficulty with money, telling the time, giving/following directions, using right and left and sequencing events. He may also be prone to losing track of turntaking, e.g. in team games or dance.
- Poor time management and organisation skills.

How can the modern languages teacher help?

- Provide number/word/rule lists etc. rather than expect the pupil to copy from the board. (Credit card holders can be useful for keeping reminders close at hand to aid memory.)
- Teach French numbers beyond 69 as discrete lexical items – don't try to explain how they work.
- Make full use of IT to support learning.
- Encourage the use of rough paper for working out.
- Check understanding at regular intervals.
- Offer a framework for setting out work.
- Provide concrete, practical objects that are appropriate for the pupil's age.
- Allow extra time for tasks including assessments and examinations.

> **Further information**
>
> www.bdadyslexia.org.uk/dyslexic/dyscalculia

Dyspraxia

Dyspraxia is a common developmental disorder that affects fine and gross motor coordination and may also affect speech. The pattern of coordination difficulties will vary from person to person and will affect participation and functioning in everyday life as well as in school.

Main characteristics

- difficulty in co-ordinating movements, making pupils appear clumsy
- difficulty with handwriting and drawing, throwing and catching
- confusion between left and right
- difficulty in following sequences and multiple instructions
- weak grasp of spatial concepts: in, above, behind, etc.
- may misinterpret situations, take things literally
- limited social skills resulting in frustration and irritability
- possible articulation difficulties

How can the modern languages teacher help?

- Be sensitive to the pupil's limitations in games and practical/outdoor activities and plan tasks to enable success.
- Limit the amount of writing expected.
- Ask the pupil questions to check his understanding of instructions/tasks.
- Use concrete objects to model prepositions, e.g. a soft toy on/in/under/ behind a box.
- Pass a soft toy/ball round a circle or get pupils to nominate who is to answer the next question rather than throw the object, or use a random name generator like the one found on the classtools.net website, or the 'Decide now' app.
- Check the pupil's seating position to encourage good presentation (both feet resting on the floor, desk at elbow height and ideally with a sloping surface on which to work).

> **Further information**
>
> Dyspraxia Foundation   01462 455 016   www.dyspraxiafoundation.org.uk

Speech, language and communication difficulties (SLCD)

Pupils with speech, language and communication difficulties have problems that affect the full range of communication and the development of skills may be significantly delayed. Such difficulties are very common in young children but most problems are resolved during the primary years. Problems that persist beyond the transfer to secondary school will be more severe and will have a significant effect on self-esteem, and personal and social relationships. The development of literacy skills is also likely to be affected. Even where pupils learn to decode, they may not understand what they have read. Sign language and symbols offer pupils an additional method of communication. Pupils with speech, language and communication difficulties cover the whole range of academic abilities.

Main characteristics

- **Speech difficulties**
  Difficulties with expressive language may involve problems in articulation and the production of speech sounds, or in coordinating the muscles that control speech. Pupils may have a stammer or some other form of dysfluency.

- **Language/communication difficulties**
  Receptive language impairments lead to difficulty in understanding other people. Pupils may use words incorrectly with inappropriate grammatical patterns, have a reduced vocabulary, or find it hard to recall words and express ideas. Some pupils will also have difficulty using and understanding eye contact, facial expression, gesture and body language.

How can the modern languages teacher help?

- Gather information about the pupil (perhaps via the SENCO) and talk to the pupil himself about strategies to support him in your subject.
- Use visual supports such as objects, pictures, symbols.
- Use the pupil's name when addressing him to alert him to a question or instruction.
- Give one instruction at a time, using short sentences.
- Give pupils time to respond before repeating a question.
- Provide a good model of spoken language and rephrase the pupil's response where appropriate: 'I think you are saying that . . . .'
- Make sure pupils understand what they have to do before expecting them to start a task.
- Pair with a work/subject buddy.
- Give access to a computer or other IT equipment appropriate to the subject.
- Give written homework instructions.

Further information

I CAN	0845 225 4073 or 020 7843 2552	www.ican.org.uk
AFASIC	0300 666 9410 (Helpline)	www.afasic.org.uk

Tourette's syndrome (TS)

Tourette's syndrome is a neurological disorder characterised by 'tics': involuntary rapid or sudden movements or sounds that are frequently repeated. There is a wide range of severity of the condition with some people having no need to seek medical help whilst others have a socially disabling condition. The tics can be suppressed for a short time but will be more noticeable when the pupil is anxious or excited.

Main characteristics

Physical tics range from simple blinking or nodding through more complex movements and conditions such as echopraxia (imitating actions seen) or copropraxia (repeatedly making obscene gestures).

Vocal tics may be as simple as throat clearing or coughing but can progress to be as extreme as echolalia (the repetition of what was last heard) or coprolalia (the repetition of obscene words).

TS itself causes no behavioural or educational problems but pupils may also have other associated disorders such as attention deficit hyperactivity disorder (ADHD) or obsessive compulsive disorder (OCD).

How can the modern languages teacher help?

- Establish a good rapport with the pupil.
- Talk to the class about TS and establish an understanding and tolerant ethos.
- Agree an 'escape route' signal should the tics become overwhelming for the pupil, or disruptive for the rest of the class.
- Allow pupil to sit at the back of the room to be less obvious.
- Give access to a computer to reduce the need for handwriting.
- Allow for non-verbal responses to questions, e.g. use of mini-whiteboards, sorting pictures into a correct sequence, simple puzzles like Tarsia.
- Make sure the pupil is not teased or bullied.
- Be alert for signs of anxiety or depression.

Further information

Tourettes Action   UK 0300 777 8427   www.tourettes-action.org.uk
                     (Helpdesk)

Appendix 1.4 Individual case studies

Read the case studies which follow. There are suggestions for classroom strategies here but there is also space for you to add your own.

Kuli Y8, Hearing impairment

Kuli has profound hearing loss. He has some hearing in his right ear but is heavily reliant on visual cues ranging from lip reading to studying body language and facial expression to get the gist and tone of what people are saying. He often misses crucial details. Reading is a useful alternative input and his mechanical reading skills are good, but he does not always get the full message because of language delay. He has problems with new vocabulary and with asking and responding to questions.

He follows the same timetable as the rest of his class for most of the week but he has some individual tutorial sessions with a teacher of the deaf to help with his understanding of the curriculum and to focus on his speech and language development. This is essential but it does mean that he misses some classes, so he is not always up to speed with a subject.

He has a good sense of humour but appreciates visual jokes more than ones which are language based. He is very literal and is puzzled by all sorts of idioms. He was shocked when he heard that someone had been 'painting the town red' as he thought this was an act of vandalism! Even when he knows what he wants to say he does not always have the words or structures to communicate accurately what he knows.

Everyone is very pleasant and quite friendly to him but he is not really part of any group and quite often misunderstands what other children are saying. He has a learning assistant, which again marks him out as different. He gets quite frustrated because he always has ideas that are too complex for his expressive ability. He can be very sulky and has temper tantrums.

Strategies

- Kuli needs to know what is coming up in the next few lessons so he can prepare the vocabulary and get some sense of the main concepts and thus be able to follow what is being said.
- A good TA will find ways of displaying information visually using drawings, pictures, signs, symbols, sign language, mime and animations on the computer, etc.
- ....
....
....
- ....
....
....
- ....
....
....

Bhavini Y9, Visual impairment

Bhavini has very little useful sight. She uses a stick to get around the large comprehensive school where she is a pupil, and some of the other children make cruel comments about this which she finds very hurtful. She also wears glasses with thick lenses which she hates. On more than one occasion, she has been knocked over in the corridor, but she insists that these incidents were accidents and that she is not being bullied. However, her sight is so poor she could not recognise anyone who picked on her.

She has a certain amount of specialist equipment such as talking scales in cookery, a CCTV for textbooks and is always conscious of being different. Her classmates accept her, but she is very cut off as she does not make eye contact or see well enough to find people she knows to sit with at break. She spends a lot of time hanging around the support area. Her form tutor has tried to get other children to take her under their wing or to escort her to humanities, which is in another building, but this has bred resentment. She has friends outside school at the local Phab club and has taken part in regional VI athletics tournaments, but she opts out of sport at school if she can. Some of the teachers are concerned about health and safety issues and there has been talk about her being disapplied from science.

She has a reading age approximately three years behind her chronological age and spells phonetically. Many of the teaching strategies which are used to make learning more interesting disadvantage her. The lively layout of her French book with cartoons and speech bubbles is a nightmare. Even if she has a page on her CCTV or has a photocopy of the text enlarged she cannot track which bit goes where. At the end of one term she turned up at the support base asking for some work to do because 'they're all watching videos'.

Strategies

- Her isolation is the key factor and needs addressing most urgently.
- She needs to be put in groups with different pupils who will not overwhelm her.
- She needs work on spelling – core vocabulary and spelling patterns which are not phonic.
- ....
....
....
- ....
....
....
- ....
....
....

Megan Y10, Wheelchair user

Nicknamed Little Miss Angry, everyone knows when Megan is around! She is very outgoing, loud and tough. No one feels sorry for her – they wouldn't dare! Megan has spina bifida and needs personal care as well as educational support. She has upset a number of the less experienced classroom assistants who find her a real pain. Some of the teachers like her because she is very sparky. If she likes a subject, she works hard – or at least she did until this year.

Megan has to be up very early for her parents to help get her ready for school before the bus comes at 7.50 am. She lives out of town and is one of the first to be picked up and one of the last to be dropped off, so she has a longer school day than many of her classmates. Tiredness can be a problem as everything takes her so long to do and involves so much effort.

Now she is 15 she has started working towards her GCSEs and has the potential to get several A to Cs, particularly in maths and sciences. She is intelligent, but is in danger of becoming disaffected because everything is so much harder for her than for other children. Recently she has lost her temper with a teacher, made cruel remarks to a very sensitive child and turned her wheelchair round so she sat with her back to a supply teacher. She has done no homework for the last few weeks, saying that she doesn't see the point as 'no one takes a crip seriously'.

Strategies

- Urgent support is needed to minimise the physical effort involved in writing and recording.
- The school needs to establish ground rules about behaviour.
- Rotate TAs so Megan doesn't wear them out.
- ....
  ....
  ....
- ....
  ....
  ....
- ....
  ....
  ....

Steven Y8, Emotional, behavioural, social difficulties

'Stevie' is a real charmer – sometimes! He is totally inconsistent: one day, he is full of enthusiasm; the next day, he is very tricky and he needs to be kept on target. He thrives on attention. In primary school, he spent a lot of time sitting by the teacher's desk and seemed to enjoy feeling special. If he sat there he would get on with his work, but as soon as he moved to sit with his friends he wanted to make sure he was the centre of attention.

Steven sometimes seems lazy, looking for the easy way out, but at other times he is quite dynamic and has lots of bright ideas. He can't work independently and has a very short attention span. No one has very high expectations of him and he is not about to prove them wrong.

Some of the children don't like him because he can be a bully but really he is not nasty. He is a permanent lieutenant for some of the tougher boys and does things to win their approval. He is a thief but mostly he takes silly things, designed to annoy rather than for any monetary value. He was found with someone's library ticket and stole one shoe from the changing rooms during PE.

Since his mother has taken up with a new partner, there has been a deterioration in behaviour and Steven has also been cautioned by police after stealing from a local DIY store. He has just been suspended for throwing a chair at a teacher but, staff suspect, this was because he was on a dare. He certainly knows how to get attention.

Strategies

- Steven needs a structured programme with lots of rewards – certificates, merits, etc.
- Praise to overcome negative self-image.
- ....
....
....
- ....
....
....
- ....
....
....

Matthew Y9, Cognitive and learning difficulties

Matt is a very passive boy. He has no curiosity, and no strong likes or dislikes. One teacher said, 'He's the sort of boy who says yes to everything to avoid further discussion but I sometimes wonder if he understands anything.'

He is quite a loner. He knows all the children and does not feel uncomfortable with any of them, but is always on the margins. Often in class he sits and does nothing, just stares into space. He is no trouble and indeed if there is any kind of conflict, he absents himself or ignores it. No one knows very much about him as he never volunteers any information. In French, he once said that he had a dog, and one teacher has seen him on the local common with a terrier, but no one is sure if it is his.

He does every piece of work as quickly as possible to get it over with. His work is messy and there is no substance to anything he does, which makes it hard for teachers to suggest a way forward, or indeed to find anything to praise. Matthew often looks a bit grubby and is usually untidy. He can be quite clumsy and loses things regularly but does not bother to look for them. He does less than the minimum.

He is in a low set for maths but stays in the middle. He has problems with most humanities subjects because he has no empathy and no real sense of what is required. When the class went to visit a museum for their work on the Civil War, he was completely unmoved. To him, it was just another building, and he could not really link it with the work they had done in history.

Strategies

- Involve him in pair work with a livelier pupil who will 'gee' him up a bit.
- Set up some one-to-one sessions with a TA where he is pushed to respond.
- Get him using technology to improve the appearance of his work, perhaps in a homework club after school.
- ....
  ....
  ....
- ....
  ....
  ....
- ....
  ....
  ....

Susan Y10, Complex difficulties, autistic spectrum disorder

Susan is a tall, very attractive girl who has been variously labelled as having Asperger's and 'cocktail party syndrome'. She talks fluently but usually about something totally irrelevant. She is very charming and her language is sometimes quite sophisticated, but her understanding and ability to use language for school work operate at a much lower level. Her reading is excellent on some levels, but she cannot draw inferences from the printed word. If you ask her questions about what she has read, she looks blank, echoes what you have said, looks puzzled, or changes the subject – something she is very good at.

She finds relationships quite difficult. She is very popular, especially with the boys in her class. They think she is a laugh. There have been one or two problems with older boys in the school. Her habit of standing too close to people and her over-familiarity in manner have led to misunderstandings which have upset her badly. Her best friend Laura is very protective of her and tries to mother her, to the extent of doing some of her work for her so she won't get into trouble.

Her work is limited. In art, all her pictures look the same – very small cramped drawings – and she does not like to use paint because 'it's messy'. She finds it very hard to relate to the wider world and sees everything in terms of her own experience. The class has been studying *Macbeth* and she has not moved beyond saying, 'I don't believe in witches and ghosts'.

Some teachers think she is being wilfully stupid or not paying attention. She seems to be attention seeking as she is very poor at turn taking and shouts out in class if she thinks of something to say or wants to know how to spell a word. When she was younger, she used to retreat under the desk when she was upset and had to be coaxed out. She is still easily offended and cannot bear being teased. She has an answer for everything and, while it may not be sensible or reasonable, there is always an underlying logic.

Strategies

- Susan should be taught to count to 20 before opening her mouth.
- She should be given writing frames and model answers she can base her work on.
- There should be discussion of social issues, body language, appropriate behaviour, etc.
- ....
....
....
- ....
....
....
- ....
....
....

Jenny Y7, Down's syndrome

Jenny is a very confident child who has been cherished and encouraged by her mother and older brothers and sisters. She is very assertive and is more than capable of dealing with spiteful comments: 'I don't like it when you call me names. You're cruel and I hate you', but this assertiveness can lead to obstinacy. She is prone to telling teachers that they are wrong!

She is good at reading and writing but her work is sometimes unimaginative and pedestrian. She enjoys maths and biology but finds the rest of the science curriculum hard going. She has started to put on weight and tries to avoid PE. She has persuaded her mother to provide a note saying that she tires easily but staff know that she is a bundle of energy and is an active member of an amateur theatre group which performs musicals. She has a good singing voice and enjoys dancing.

She went to a local nursery and primary school and fitted in well. She always had someone to sit next to and was invited to all the best birthday parties. Teachers and other parents frequently praised her, and she felt special.

Now, in secondary school, everything has changed. Some of her friends from primary school have made new friendships and don't want to spend so much time with her. She is very hurt by this and feels excluded. She is also struck by how glamorous some of the older girls look, and this has made her more self-conscious.

Strategies

- Talk to Jenny's parents about diet and exercise, and find a way of making her feel more attractive.
- Encourage new groupings in class so she gets to meet other children from different feeder schools.
- ....
....
....
- ....
....
....
- ....
....
....

Harry Y7, Dyslexia

Harry is a very anxious little boy and, although he has now started at secondary school, he still seems to be a 'little boy'. His parents have been very concerned about his slow progress in reading and writing and arranged for a dyslexia assessment when he was eight years old. They also employ a private tutor who comes to the house for two hours per week, and they spend time each evening and at weekends hearing him read and working on phonics with him.

Harry expresses himself well orally, using words which are very sophisticated and adult. His reading is improving (RA 8.4) but his handwriting and spelling are so poor that it is sometimes difficult to work out what he has written. He doesn't just confuse 'b' and 'd' but also 'h' and 'y', 'p' and 'b'. Increasingly, he uses only a small bank of words that he knows he can spell.

His parents want him to be withdrawn from French on the grounds that he has enough problems with English. The French teacher reports that Harry is doing well with his comprehension and spoken French and is one of the more able children in the class.

Some staff get exasperated with Harry as he is quite clumsy, seems to be in a dream half the time, and cannot remember a simple sequence of instructions. He has difficulty telling left from right and so is often talking about the wrong diagram in a book or is out of step in dance classes. 'He's just not trying,' said one teacher, while others think he needs to 'grow up a bit'.

He is popular with the girls in his class and recently has made friends with some of the boys in the choir. Music is Harry's great passion, but his parents are not willing for him to learn an instrument at the moment.

Strategies

- Find out how he has learnt things and see if similar strategies would work in the classroom.
- Investigate the possibility of using a computer with a spellchecker at home and school to cope with orthographic and spelling difficulties.
- ....
  ....
  ....
- ....
  ....
  ....
- ....
  ....
  ....

Appendix 1.5 Case study: Ramsey Grammar School, Isle of Man

We are a very fortunate school in that many of our SEND students come to MFL lessons. I am by no means an expert but here are some of the things that have worked in my classroom.

The most important thing is a really warm and safe environment where mistakes are welcomed and nobody is laughed at for trying. This is absolutely essential for all students but especially those with learning difficulties.

Consistency of discipline. All students like to know where the line is but I think this is even more so for SEND students. Autistic children like to be in the same seat every lesson. I usually seat them near me. I taught a severely autistic child last year. I had taught him in Y7 and when he came back to me in Y10 he wanted to sit in exactly the same place as in Y7 – fortunately I'd put him there!

In terms of dyslexics I tend to work on all aspects of language more than writing. When it comes to writing I worry less about their spelling. A number of our SEND students use an iPad to help them in class so use text to voice for reading and voice to text for writing. It's not always perfect and I always insist that they check back for mistakes if they can. We have a policy of having a vocabulary test every other week. The pass mark is 7/10 albeit that five questions are from FL into English and another five the other way. I am pretty generous with the marking of my dyslexic students' work.

With autistic students I spend a lot of time 1:1 with them outside the lesson ensuring understanding of homework and classwork. The boy I was talking about above had a stammer. I eventually, after much to-ing and fro-ing with the exam board, managed to get him extra time for his speaking exam. He was most relaxed when he spoke whilst walking and stammered less, so I would ask the question into the iPad and he would then take it and walk around to give his answer.

In all of this, I think it's important to find what works for the students in front of you. A kind, firm, caring approach often yields the best results. I think being as flexible as you can be in your teaching and trying to integrate students as much as humanly possible into class is the best way forward. Last year we did 'secret Santa' with my Y11 class. My autistic student didn't want to join in, so all the other students asked if he would like to be Santa and give out the presents. They brought a Santa hat in for him and everything – they even bought him some chocolates. He was totally made up!

The autistic student from last year gained a grade C at GCSE in French and a B in Spanish. I teach his brother this year who is also on the spectrum but he functions at a much higher level – he will get an A!

Appendix 2.1 Worksheet design

A poor worksheet

Plan a day out

Pizza Lumière.

Tél. 895 54 87

Ouvert tous les jours

"C'est si bon!"

Restaurant Mirabeau

Tél 679.30.33 Plat du jour 20E; Fermé dimanche

CHEZ PIERRE

Tél 583 79.30. Déjeuner, dîner, souper. Fermé lundi et mardi.
Fruits des mers et crustaces

Musée de l'Armée, Hôtel des invalides
Tél. 55 97 30
Ouvert tous les jours 10h á 19h Entrée 6 E
14h á 17 h films sur les deux guerres mondiales

"Merveilleux!"

What makes this hard to read?

- the irregular spacing between words and lines
- the right justified margin
- the range of fonts
- the range of font sizes
- the text wrapped around an image
- the use of italics and bold

- the mixture of capital letters and lower case
- the activity is not explained.

These features would disadvantage a learner with poor visual tracking skills. A pupil with dyslexia, learning difficulties or lacking confidence would struggle with the layout . . . and that's before they start trying to make sense of the words! What are they supposed to do other than read the text?

A good worksheet

Lisez le texte suivant. Répondez aux questions.

Salut!

Je m'appelle Maria . . . Comment t'appelles tu? Je suis fille unique et j'ai quatorze ans. Je suis canadienne. Ma mère est australienne mais mon père est canadien. D'où viens tu? Je suis en troisième, c'est très difficile parce qu'il y a beaucoup de devoirs.

Pour mes passetemps j'aime parler au téléphone, faire du shopping, lire des livres romantiques, regarder des films d'horreur. J'aime aussi la natation et le soccer.

Ma musique preferée est le hip-hop et le rap.

Bon, maintenent je dois aller à mon prochain cours.

Au revoir~!

Maria

	Vrai?	Faux?
Elle est espagnole	❑	❑
Elle aime la natation	❑	❑
Elle regard les films romantiques	❑	❑

What makes this a good worksheet?

- The use of two fonts: one for text, one for activities/instructions.
- Short lines and 1.5 line spacing helps with tracking.
- The activity is clear so the pupil knows what to do.

Appendix 3.1 Pictures

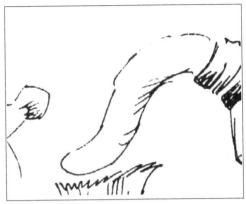 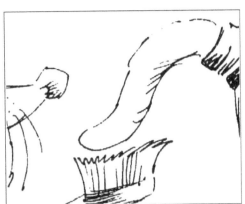

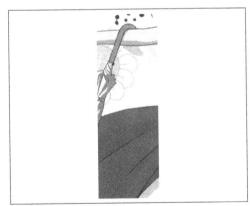 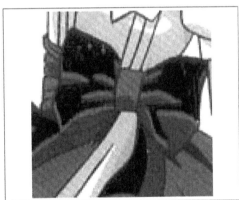

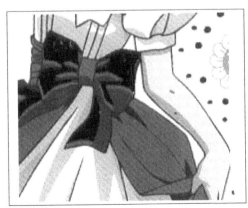 

Appendix 3.2 Useful resources*

Websites

www.voki.com

www.blabberize.com

www.storybird.com

www.stripgenerator.com

www.toondoo.com

www.glogster.com

www.padlet.com

www.classtools.net

www.makebeliefscomix.com

www.linoit.com

www.rachelhawkes.com

www.jamesnottingham.co.uk/learning-pit

www.qr-code-generator.com

www.all-literature.wikidot.com

www.clil4teachers.pbworks.com

www.nicurriculum.org.uk

www.memrise.com

www.goanimate.com

Apps

Duolingo

Busuu

iNigma (QR code reader)

Morfo

Croakit

Show me

Evernote

Puppet Pals

Lerni

Memrise

Babbel
Learn 50 Languages
Rosetta Stone
SayHi!
Yakit4Kids
ExplainEverything
Speakpipe
Tellagami

Note

* As accessed July 2016

Appendix 3.3 Starter activities

Starter activities tune pupils into the language and get them thinking and working. Keep them short. Beware any starters that involve anagrams or rearranging letters within part of a word. These are not suitable for pupils with dyslexia or others who have poor visual spelling skills.

Wordworms to recognise words and improve vocabulary

JeanetPierrerentrentchezeuxaprèsunemoisdevacancesàlacampagne

Jean et Pierre rentrent chez eux après une mois de vacances à la campagne.

Reorganise words within a sentence to develop a sense of syntax

Die Ferien:

anschauen / Markt / den / ich / will /
wollen / Fahrräder / wir / leihen

Match up words and topics to recognise contexts (look for key words)

Palabras	*Lugares*
1. No me siento bien.	a. el banco
2. La cuenta por favor.	b. la piscina
3. Tiene usted un plan de la ciudad?	c. la farmacia
4. A qué hora empieza la pelicula?	d. el restaurante
5. Querría cambiar dinero.	e. información y turismo
6. El agua está fría.	f. el cine

(Answers 1c, 2d, 3e, 4f, 5a, 6b)

Find the odd one out to practise grammar/vocabulary

rot/grau/klein/gelb   (*klein* not a colour)

Allemagne anglais chinois espagnol   (*Allemagne* country not nationality)

singen/zwei/kaufen/zahlen   (*zwei* not a verb)

correos buzón sellos reloj   (*reloj* not to do with post office)

Fill in missing letters to practise spelling and revise vocabulary

Strong verbs with *haben*:

b- -i-nen   (beginnen)

s- -en   (sehen)

-e-men   (nehmen)

-r-n-en   (trinken)

Match beginnings and ends of sentences – reading for sense

Ich habe ein Brüder.   Sie heißen Karl, Dieter und Hans.

Ich habe eine Schwester.   Sie heißen Ingrid und Erika.

Ich habe zwei Gebrüder und ein   Er heißt Hans.
Halbbrüder.

Ich habe zwei Schwestern.   Sie heißen Michael und Elisabeth.

Ich habe ein Brüder und eine   Sie heißt Gisela.
Halbschwester.

Find the grammatical mistakes

Adjectival agreements:

Marie a perdu les chemises blanc.   (blanches)

J'ai acheté des chaussures verts.   (vertes)

La jupe noir est trop courts.   (noire, courte)

Odd sound out to practise pronunciation and to match sound to spelling

Michelle; chercher; chez; glace; riche   (glace)

quand; jusque; cher; pourquoi; quelle   (cher)

bois; noir; doux; choisir; pourquoi   (doux)

jambon; chaise; bonjour; bijou; ajouter   (chaise)

Appendix 3.4 French vocabulary work

1 Adjectives

1. You are working on adjectives to describe people. The class has a core of 20 basic adjectives.

aimable	amusant	bavard	beau	charmant
chic	dangereux	difficile	drôle	ennuyeux
génial	gentil	honnête	intelligent	joli
mignon	paresseux	poli	sportif	sympathique

Choose two of the following activities.

(a) Choose a character from a soap. (Give them one if the decision making is going to go on too long.) Pick out all the adjectives which apply to him or her. Find three other adjectives which could apply to that person.
(b) Draw a wanted poster. *Avez-vous vu cet homme/cette femme?*
(c) Pick three different people in the class. Create a form – *nom /âge/ cheveux/yeux/caractère* and fill in a form with four adjectives for each.
(d) Write a series of five questions which can be answered with 'yes' or 'no'. *Ton frère est parasseux? Est-il sportif?*

2. *Les smileys*

This activity was created by Gail Haythorne of Woldingham School in Surrey.

Vous chattez? Trouvez la bonne image pour chaque adjectif!

1.	:-D	triste
2.	:-0	très triste

3.	;-j	étonné/étonnée
4.	>:->	rebelle
5.	:c	fâché/fâchée
6.	:-T	effrayé/effrayée
7.	:*(	honnête
8.	:-x	bavard/bavarde
9.	:-P	heureux/heureuse
10.	=:O	jeune
11.	0:)	impatient/impatiente
12.	:()	ennuyé/ennuyée
13.	:0)	timide
14.	:-@	sarcastique
15.	~:)	irrité/irritée
16.	I-0	méchant/méchante
17.	:-}	gentil/gentille
18.	:-[	embarrassé/embarrassée

Maintenant, décrivez votre famille et vos amis. Par exemple: Ma mère est heureuse et bavarde. Mon frère est souvent irrité.

Trouvez/inventez d'autres smileys. Recherchez 'emoticons' dans le site: www.about.com

Les réponses: triste 5; très triste 7; étonné 2; rebelle 9; fâché 14; effrayé 10; honnête 11; bavard 12; heureux 1; jeune 15; impatient 6; ennuyé 16; timide 8; sarcastique 3; irrité 18; méchant 4; gentil 13; embarrassé 17

2 Remplissez les blancs

Cher/Chère ———

Ca va? Moi, ça va bien. Aujourd'hui je te parle un peu de mon collège. Mon collège s'appelle ——————. Il y a ——— élèves. Moi, je suis en ———.

J'aime/je déteste le collège. J'aime (anglais, histoire etc.) ——— et ——— ——, mais je n'aime pas ——— ou ——— (anglais, histoire, etc.) parce que ——————.

Et toi, qu'est-ce que tu aimes au collège? Tu aimes les profs? Écris-moi bientôt.

_____

3 Qu'est-ce que tu peux voir?

Appendix 3.5 Testing German vocabulary

Make word searches for different levels of ability. (There are a number of sources for generating word squares which can be found by using an Internet search engine.)

e	d	y	h	h	d	t	h	b	t
e	f	n	v	o	k	l	a	i	u
s	l	q	a	r	t	h	a	k	r
e	u	u	a	r	n	e	i	w	m
l	g	m	t	h	t	n	l	q	w
u	h	w	o	m	o	s	w	a	f
h	a	f	l	e	h	c	r	i	k
c	f	g	m	s	t	a	d	t	h
s	e	g	r	u	b	u	n	a	w
y	n	s	p	q	h	z	y	i	e

bahnhof	kirche	strand
burg	markt	turm
flughafen	schule	wald
hotel	see	
kino	stadt	

Differentiate word squares by:

- size of square (a smaller square with fewer words for an easier puzzle)
- size and style of print; upper or lower case letters
- checklist (provide the list of words to be found and matched – in English or German)
- orientation (letters running backwards or diagonally make the task more difficult, as do overlapping words).

Also, ask the pupils to make up their own word search.

Appendix 5.1 Guidance for teaching assistants

Golden rules

- Help pupils to succeed but allow them to fail.
- In language learning, everyone learns from their mistakes.
- Avoid highly idiomatic English. Idioms are confusing for non-native speakers of English and for pupils with certain language disorders.

Personal information

- Build on and respect personal information and experience.
- In MFL classes you will learn a lot about people's identity, family – or lack of it – preferences, hobbies and lifestyle.
- MFL is very person-centred. Listen, learn and use this knowledge to foster closer relationships with the child.
- Beware differences in culture. Use a range of examples rather than ones which assume a particular background or experience. Not all pupils want shopping, music, reading or football as their hobbies.

Encourage pupils to participate in class but be aware of individual differences

- Don't just talk: draw and mime as well.
- Many pupils benefit from both seeing and hearing language.
- Try to get each pupil to participate in spoken work; ask questions but increase the time you wait for an answer for slower thinkers and less confident pupils.
- Challenge the louder and more dominant pupils.
- Don't assume that students who don't talk don't know the material.
- Think about talking to very quiet and very loud pupils outside class.

References and further information

Anstee, P. (2011) *Differentiation pocket book*. Alresford: Teachers' Pocketbooks.

Caldwell, E. (2002) 'A difficulty, *oui*, but a deficit, *non*', *TES Scotland*, 10 May.

Children and Families Act 2014. www.legislation.gov.uk/ukpga/2014/6/contents/enacted

DfE (2014) *National curriculum and assessment from September 2014: Information for schools*. London: DfE Publications. www.gov.uk/government/uploads/system/uploads/attachment_data/file/358070/NC_assessment_quals_factsheet_Sept_update.pdf

DfE (2015a) *SEND Code of Practice*. London: DfE Publications.

DfE (2015b) *DfE Statistical First Release*, July. www.gov.uk/government/uploads/system/uploads/attachment_data/file/440577/Text_SFR21-2015.pdf

DfES (1999) *Reducing the bureaucratic burden on teachers*. Referred to in: www.teachers.org.uk/.../sixth_form_colleges-njc_joint_guidance_on_bureaucracydec1999

DfES (2002) *Languages for all: Languages for life, a strategy for England*. www.dfes.gov.uk/languagesstrategy

DfES (2005) *Key Stage 2 Framework for Languages*. London: DfE Publications.

Dweck, C. (2012) *Mindset: How you can fulfil your potential.* London: Robinson.

Equality Act 2010: Guidance. www.gov.uk/guidance/equality-act-2010-guidance

Erler, L. and Prince, J. (2012) *Sounds and words: Supporting language learning through phonics*. Reading: CfBT Education Trust.

Howes, B. (2001) 'Those French people are really clever', *Special Children*, June.

Jones, J. and Wiliam, D. (2008) *Modern foreign languages inside the black box: Assessment for learning in the modern foreign languages classroom.* London: GL Assessment.

Lovey, J. (2002) *Supporting special educational needs in secondary school classrooms*. London: David Fulton Publishers.

Ofsted (2003) *Good assessment practice in modern foreign languages* (HMI 1478). London: DfES.

Riener, C. and Willingham, D. (2010) 'The myth of learning styles', *Change: The magazine of higher learning*, September–October. www.changemag.org/archives/back%20issues/september-october%202010/the-myth-of-learning-full.html

Tinsley, T. and Comfort, T. (2012) *Lessons from abroad: International review of primary languages*. Reading: CfBT Education Trust.

Vygotsky, L. (1930) *Tool and symbol in child development*. www.marxists.org/archive/vygotsky/works/1934/tool-symbol.htm

Wilson, D. (2003) 'Accessing the secondary school curriculum'. SENDcoforumlists.becta.org.uk/pipermail/SENDco-forum/2003-July/032283.html

Websites

http://maximisingtas.co.uk
www.skillsforschools.org.uk/roles_in_schools/teaching-assistant
www.voki.com
www.blabberize.com
www.storybird.com
www.stripgenerator.com
www.toondoo.com
www.glogster.com
www.padlet.com
www.classtools.net
www.makebeliefscomix.com
www.linoit.com
www.rachelhawkes.com
www.jamesnottingham.co.uk/learning-pit
www.qr-code-generator.com
www.all-literature.wikidot.com
www.clil4teachers.pbworks.com
www.nicurriculum.org.uk
www.memrise.com
www.goanimate.com

Apps

Duolingo
Busuu
iNigma (QR code reader)
Morfo
Croakit
Show me
Evernote
Puppet Pals
Lerni
Memrise
Babbel
Learn 50 Languages
Rosetta Stone
SayHi!
Yakit4Kids
ExplainEverything
Speakpipe
Tellagami

Index